Little Book —
Big Questions

by Carlton Burrell

Dorrance Publishing Co
585 Alpha Drive
Pittsburgh, PA 15238
Visit our website at *www.dorrancebookstore.com*

ISBN: 978-1-6491-3517-9
eISBN: 978-1-6491-3934-4

Dedicated to the world.

The Awakening

It's a subject nobody wants to talk about, except reluctantly, and he's no different. He'd been postponing this conversation for years until recently when it dawned on him that there were certain things that just couldn't be ignored. This was one of them! It's as common as life itself, in fact one could say there's an uneasy resignation to it and an attendant sense of helplessness that is frightfully sobering. Wherever life goes, it follows, stalking, always stalking, until, poof, it strikes.

Over a lifetime, Mr. I.M. Everyman had been taught and reminded about the dangers of procrastinating, yet somehow it seemed not to have resonated with him. Not so now, no! No! No! Multiple nos. He'd had a long time to reflect and to put things in perspective, especially on an overcast day like this, a day he feels a nexus with, a day which in an uncanny way mirrors his own life.

Here's a guy who'd seen some of his closest, dearest, most loved and cherished relatives, friends, associates, neighbors, and "others" stolen away. They were no longer around, and notwithstanding his wishing, hoping, praying, asking, and looking for signs of their re-appearance, it's as if they'd vanished from the face of the earth; it's almost as if they never existed. All they are, are just memories. Where did they go? he wondered, puzzled. As far as he knows, none of those who'd "migrated" to parts unknown communicated with him, and he found that troubling, and the more he thought about it, the more perplexed he became, especially in view of the promise they'd made to be in contact with each other, no matter what. Where did they all go? Gosh darn it, maybe he wasn't as close to them, any of them as he thought, and so he chided himself, even as he continued to reflect on the situation, concluding as anyone so desperate for answers would, that must be it! What else could it be? There's nothing else he could think of that made sense to him, and when you think about it, it's almost impossible for everybody to have forgotten the promise they'd made, and such a solemn one too, huh, huh! That's too much of a coincidence. Yes! They weren't as close, that's the obvious answer. They weren't as "tight" as he believed. Gosh! What a shame, "a crying shame," he'd say, yet what struck him even more as he thought about these losses is the mystery of it all. This is a poignant moment for him.

He remembers there was a time, not too long ago, when he never thought the term "senior citizen" would or could be a reference to him, and as preposterous as it sounds, he somehow saw himself retaining his youthful self forever. He was in denial! For sure he was. Somehow he never pictured himself hunched over, slowing down, or even using a cane or having any of the limitations and/or mannerisms of the elderly. That was for other people, not him, and that despite the fact that he saw older folks every single day. Notwithstanding his reluctance, the passage of time and all the other criteria used to make such a determination forced him to admit that he was, and that fact brought his own mortality into sharper focus, so much so that whenever he looked at himself in the mirror, he felt he was seeing the prelude, the fore-runner if you will, in fact the very outline of death making its rapid and purposeful approach. Call it paranoia or whatever you want, that's how he felt, and so day by day, he became more attentive to himself and noted among other things, the failing eyesight, the constant pain, the receding hairline, the shrinkages, the creeping loss of memory, the loss of hearing, the loss of physical strength, the shortness of breath, the deepening lines on his face and elsewhere, the loss of balance, and most of all, becoming impotent. This latter phenomenon he calls "the first death," To him living had gone into remission, as one of the main joys for living, if not the main joy was missing, taken away abruptly and unceremoniously. Gone forever! He took it very hard as these and a plethora of other death-like traits had become permanent and unwanted fixtures in his life, and he hated that. This situation led him to peer increasingly into mirrors, any mirror, anywhere, and there were times, more often than not, when he saw his own reflection and recoiled. Such times he'd mutter under his breath, "What the hell!" or "What is this?" or "What's happening to me?" or "I can't believe this!" What he saw was a shadow of his former self, the opposite of what he used to be, and he didn't like it, not even for a second. Aging had been unkind to him. There was no other way to put it, and it was hard for him to reconcile himself to the reality that what he saw was the "new" I.M. He was barely recognizable even to himself, and it made him sad and more at odds with the idea that age was just "some" number. To him it was much more. For one the transformation was a shocker, however, he soon realized that this was a process one had to go through if one lived long enough. Like it or not, that's the stark reality, a reality he found hard to accept.

In his mind, that's confirmation enough to suggest he and death were on a collision course. This he called the "second death," and this is permanent as far as he could tell. This is the one, the feared one, the one that nobody wants to talk about, the one that some people call "the big one," the one that has finality written all over it. He looked back, all the way to his school days, and wondered if the bard was right in his seeming denunciation of life's glorification." Was he? There's plausibility, no question, and it struck a chord with him, but he was still hoping for something else, some other explanation perhaps. What he's sure of though is that he wants his life to be nothing short of exceptional, and so far it was anything but. He also knows that no time is guaranteed for him to fulfill his quest for a better explanation about life, and that's why he wants to know what he wants to know right now before it's too late. He agonizes over the fact that he doesn't know if life will continue as the religionists or the evolutionists proclaim. Which? he asks, or is there a middle ground, and if so, what is it? He's confused and he doesn't believe he should be, especially in a matter of such importance as man's future. He strongly feels that there should be no guesswork or grounds for speculation. No, no, no, there should absolutely be no room for wild theories, instead there should be certainty, and he makes no apology for having that belief. All he's seeking is clarity. What's more he believes his demand for it is just, and as such, he feels even more driven to search for supportive and compelling evidence to point him, and hopefully, others to the right conclusion, and that's a vow he intends to keep.

The very notion that there's an after-life fascinates him, and the depiction of such by religious scholars makes it worthy of even closer scrutiny. What bothers him though is whether the same people who told him about Santa Claus and the Tooth Fairy and other such characters can be trusted to tell him the truth about the future. Can they substantiate their conclusions and clearly enunciate what informs such conclusions? Can they? Do they have that kind of insight and the integrity to match?

Just in his lifetime, he'd seen the metamorphosis of society to the extent where the use of cash is being phased out, the genesis of the era of driverless motor vehicles, etc., the exploration of more planets in the search for other intelligent life-forms, and so on, new forms of communication systems where privacy is a relic of the past, the development of artificial intelligence, and genderlessness becoming the new norm. These are just a sampling of some of the more striking changes taking place as we speak. Sad to say, but with all these changes, one thing remains constant, and that thing is death! And so it begs the question, is that all there is? Life, then death? Really? If so it just goes to show how temporary man's tenure is on the planet. We're all just living to die eventually.

During his formative years, he'd read the biographies of many successful people with the goal of becoming successful himself, and by his early teens, had meticulously planned his future only to see things go awry and no matter how hard he tried, he was never able to put it back together, at least not the way he intended. His life had taken a whatever happens, happens turn, but the funny thing is, this was no song, and he wasn't dancing.

It's as if circumstance or some other unknown force was steering his life one way while he wanted it to go another way. He most definitely wasn't the one guiding it. Whatever it was pushed him aside and led him wherever it wanted, and that was mostly to his detriment.

One incident he vividly recalled during that period of his life was when he'd lost the money his mother gave him to purchase some "must have" items for the home at a nearby supermarket.

What kept ringing in his ears were the words his mother said while handing over the money, "Son please be careful, this is all the money we've got." At the time, he mulled over several solutions and in an effort to find some sort of comfort and help he confided in a neighborhood friend, who happened to be in the supermarket at the time.

"Hey, man, I need your help in a bad way," he stammered as he walked nervously towards him. He told his story and tried to borrow some money, even though he knew it was a long shot. You know the expression, which tells the measures applicable for desperate times. This was such a moment. He was willing to do almost anything and even promised a fifty per cent return on investment. In that instant, he became a "whatever it takes" kinda guy. That was the measure of his desperation, but instead of the loan or at least some semblance of empathy, the so-called friend tore into him mercilessly.

He gave him a tongue lashing he never expected, and will never forget, saying among other things, "You're too damn careless, man. In fact let's not mince words here. You're a careless so and so, and I have no sympathy for you." He was livid, "You so and so you. You're a piece of you know what! And now, yes, now you have the gall to want my money, too. The cheek of it all. What you take me for, eh? You son-of-a b…h!" He said this in a taunting manner as he repeatedly tapped on his wallet pocket. He even pulled it out halfway, looked at it, and said, "No, sir, no damn way. Not a chance! Everyman, as far as I'm concerned, you ain't nothing but a long streak of misery and a waster, too. That's what you are, and if I hadn't told you so before, my bad, I'm telling you now."

He was already at a low point in his life as almost nothing he did turned out the way he'd hoped. Now this! Sometimes he wondered if he was cursed. Luckily, he had loving and understanding parents, the kind he hopes to be one day. They always referred to him endearingly as I.M., no matter the circumstance, so even after telling them what had happened, their demeanor hadn't changed. They were consoling and let him know he was still and would always be their I.M.

For a long minute, he reflected on their love and support over the years and silently made a vow that he'd somehow find a way to make it up to them, but as he does so, his mood changed.

"Damn! Double damn! Life isn't even even," he laments, and in such a depressing mood, he couldn't help but think of his many trials and tribulations, recalling especially this other time, maybe two or three years later, when he was about sixteen or seventeen-years-old. He wasn't too sure, he'd had so many mishaps over the years, it's hard to keep track. Anyway, his very persistent tormentor, Smutty Mutty as he's called but whose real name is Foreal Smut, became involved in his affairs again. Behind his back, some say he has an uncommon name, him being such a common person and all. Be that as it may, he was the guy I.M. had tried to borrow money from during the supermarket ordeal a few years back.

This time it was in the presence of a group of mostly well-wishers who showered him with adoration after he'd won a national poetry contest.

There were chants of, "Go, I.M., go." Mutty had also entered the competition, but except for the fact that the organizers named him as one of the entrants at the very introductory stage of the program, his name was never mentioned again for the duration of the event, but that didn't deter him, oh, no, if anything it emboldened him, so during a brief pause in the celebration to render aid to someone who'd fainted, he walked to the microphone, re-introduced himself, and asked for "quiet and a moment," as he put it, "to pay homage to a dear and deserving friend.

Ladies and gentlemen," he continued, "please put your hands together and give it up for…"

But the crowd was so admiring of I.M. and his achievement, they chanted, "Let him read his poem first! We want to hear it!" I.M. beamed and basked in his new-found celebrity status, then graciously obliged.

LET'S ENGAGE THE MIND
Though problems seem insurmountable
Remember solutions are possible
Just think of the great inventors
And the obstacles they overcame
So as my contribution
Here's my simple solution
Let's engage the mind y'all
Let's engage the mind
Let's engage the mind y'all
Let's engage the mind
You've heard this before I'm sure
It's nothing new it's just a review
I'm saying what you can think of
You can also do

So let me say this for emphasis
It is imperative
Let's engage the mind y'all
Let's engage the mind
Let's engage the mind y'all
Let's engage the mind
Say you can to the goals you set
Work diligently until they're met
As if you didn't know
that's also meant for me and you
so don't ever, don't ever forget
To engage the mind
Let's engage the mind y'all
Let's engage the mind
Let's engage the mind y'all
Let's engage the mind

At the end of his recitation, he bowed in acknowledgment to the appreciative audience whose whistles and cheers rang delightfully in his ears. In fact they couldn't get enough, so he had to do encores, but he didn't mind, judging from the look on his face. He was delighted, deliriously so, and wished this could go on forever.

This kinda stuff could and would make and keep him happy for a very long time, but he also knows what they say about "all good things ending." Such a pity. Still he was so moved by the crowd's response, one could well imagine him saying to himself, if this is what success means, he wants more, and if this is what being on top of your game means, he wants to stay there, and the chant, "Go, I.M., go," never sounded sweeter to him. Finally, as he said his thank "yous" again, Smutty Mutty couldn't wait to inject himself into the proceedings again.

"Please pardon my interruption again," he says. "I tried, but I just couldn't restrain myself any longer. I hope you all understand. I...I really do. It's just that I feel a compulsion to say a few words, kind words I assure you. The honoree deserves no less. I...I hope you'll be so kind as to let me..." he begs, but he didn't wait for their permission, he kept on talking. "I want you all to know that I've known this guy for a very long time, but first and foremost, I want you to know that I sincerely appreciate your dispensing with protocol in allowing me this rare opportunity to speak here today. Bless you. I appreciate the gesture. Thank you! Thank you so... so very much. Thank you from the bottom of my heart." He looked and sounded so sincere, everyone felt at ease. He smiled. "Everyman, as you can tell, I'm in a very good mood today. A celebratory mood you could say."

Cheers rang out from the crowd as they listened attentively.

"A very good mood," he repeats, "Huh! Huh! A real good mood!" and at the pronouncement of that particular statement again and again, a broad smile crossed I.M's face. He was a picture of relaxation and was feeling "dog happy." Here's someone who'd been a thorn in his side for quite some time, actually toasting him. No more nemesis! Friends! Hallelujah! What's not to smile about? The world is at peace, his world at least. He looks over to where Smutty was and thought, what a guy. It takes a big person, no, a very big person to do what he's doing. He claps his hands together as a show of solidarity. Moments like this reinforces his belief in the goodness of mankind. So wonderful. What a blessed day. He felt like hugging the guy and smiles broadly again in anticipation of what he thought would be even more pleasantries, then he heard this as Smutty curtsied.

"I.M.," he said mockingly. He'd never called him that before, in fact anything but. To be candid, it's almost always "Everyman," or when he got bolder, he used curse words beginning with, "Mother … …" "How in GOD'S name can they let you get away with something like this?" he asks. "This is so transparent." He pauses, scratches his head, shakes it from side to side, and booms, "How! What a travesty!" He turns every which way and says to the crowd, no, exhorts the crowd, "Look at him! Please look at him, I beg you. Take a good look at your hero… please! Let me tell you exactly who he is… please allow me to. He ain't nothing but a mental midget, so how do you explain this sudden rise to mental agility, huh, huh? Something is terribly wrong here. I ain't buying it. No way! No how! He's a phony! He's a fraud! Yes! I said it, and you can take that to the bank."

He turns slightly, looks directly at I.M. and says, "Can't they see what you're doing, can't they see that someone else must have written the poem for you, or you must have plagiarized someone else's work. I'm appalled," he added in a deliberately slow manner, hoping the message he wants to get across would sink in with the crowd.

"Geez, can't they?" he continued, annoyed.

"Tell them," he exhorts. "Well, my friend, since you won't, I will. It's about time you be exposed for your deception. I'm known for my kindness and for my forgiving ways as you well know, but this is too much. This time you've gone too far, Everyman. Even I have limits and I'm telling you…" he cuts his speech abruptly, pounds his right fist repeatedly in his left palm, and curses him out. He was enraged and not holding back. This was akin to waging war. Simply put, he was out for blood and lets loose. "I'm telling you right here, right now, I've reached my breaking point with you." He wags his right index finger and bellows, "I know it probably sounds cliché, but my GOD, man, who are you? Enough is enough! Stop! I know, you know, and the world needs to know that if knowledge were ink, you wouldn't have enough to make a period; if illiteracy were crime, you'd be an habitual criminal." He pauses again for effect, saw that I.M. opened his mouth and was about to respond to his tirade, so he hastily and adroitly resumed speaking again. "You," he said, "you look intelligent with your mouth closed, so pleeeaasse do us all a favor and keep it that way sir, pplleeeasse!" He looked even more intently at I.M. and said with more than a hint of scorn, "Award-winning poet my foot! Ha," he scoffed. "You son-of-a…you mother….and I want you to know that when I call you these names, I'm being very kind to you. I'm actually doing you a big favor, you mother f…bastard. Thank you," he said to the crowd when he was through speaking. Throughout the speech, there was a collective gasp. Nobody had ever heard him speak like that before.

"So passionate," they described it in the local media. This was pent up venom, nothing less. During the speech, there was mostly silence, but after there was a mad rush for the exits. People were conflicted.

His head was throbbing, his heart pounding in his chest, and he was clearly dazed by what he'd just heard and witnessed. How could this be, he wondered. This was a verbal crucifixion, nothing less. This should have been his moment to shine, instead Smutty Mutty turned what should have been a celebratory party into a roast with him as the roastee. What made matters even worse was when he saw Rita Fleet-foot, a girl they'd both dated giggling gleefully and admiringly as she looked at Smutty Mutty but with a look of utter distain whenever she would glance his way. He couldn't understand it; he was the one who treated her with respect and kindness, whereas Smutty usually verbally abused her, calling her unflattering names and doing so even while dragging her around as if she were his personal property. What a twist, ouch! Hard as he tried, he just couldn't understand the reasoning behind Smutty's verbal attack or the scorn shown by Rita. He thought she liked him, he really did, and as for Smutty, he thought their relationship was on the mend. Then again what's to understand? Who says there has to be a rational explanation? Truth be told, this is just another typical day in his life.

"All you have to be is me," he'd mumble to himself whenever things like this happened to him, and things like this happened to him all the time. He was no stranger to grief in whatever form it took, neither was he to disappointment, however, despite other awkward moments with Smutty Mutty types, he also recalled with a degree of resentment and amusement that during his constant struggles to achieve upward mobility, he'd lived in a succession of apartments where roaches were so prevalent that someone remarked that whenever he'd return from some outdoor activity or other it seemed as if the roaches formed an honor guard to greet him. In another instance, it was widely rumored that he'd been nominated for the title of farmer of the year until someone let it slip that what he farmed were roaches, so the embarrassed nominating body hastily withdrew his name.

There was also the Rollin Glee type. He was always jolly and fun to be around. Once he and I.M. were hanging out at a popular shopping mall when a very attractive girl strolled by and caught their attention.

Never a shy guy, Rollin whistled, "Tweet, tweet," but she held her head high, kept looking straight ahead, and kept on walking, and that's when Rollin said, "Repeat," and whistled again, "tweet, tweet." This time she turned her head and smiled broadly. Whatever the reason though, the Rollin Glee type situation was a rarity in his life at that time, and so he cherished such moments whenever they occurred as kids cherish Christmastime.

2

Expectation/Reality

Hope and inspiration were things he realized he needed badly, so it was not surprising that with the raft of problems besetting him, he turned to religion for comfort. Nothing else worked, he concluded bitterly, and there was nowhere else to turn, except that some words from a song "church people" regularly sang came flooding into his memory.

It said in part that if everything else failed, you should in all probability reach out to "Jesus." It felt tailor-made for him, like it was speaking to him directly. And that's exactly what he decided to do, reach out to "Jesus."

When he was younger, much younger, he remembers the Bible was not only a fixture but also a must read in his household. From it he was taught about good and bad, right from wrong, the do's and don'ts, GOD and Satan, etcetera, but at the end of it all, he was still confused, and later when he learned there were other religions with their own sets of beliefs, practices, and GODs, he became even more confused and started to question what he'd been taught over the years.

Consequently, he sought out various proponents of the Christian faith mostly, and/or any other faith so's to be enlightened, but whatever he'd been taught, his own experience didn't match up, and so he thought someone must be playing tricks on him, and "what's really going on" was the number one question on his mind. He's serious, totally, he sure wasn't playing, neither was it his intention to ridicule or malign anyone or religious group or even to influence anyone. His sole purpose was and is to learn the truth. In other words, he's seeking honest answers from whomever. Where will he go after this life, and why was he put here? That's very personal and very important to him, and he thinks these are legitimate questions that warrant honest answers. Surely, he has the right to ask, and he being here must mean something, he reasons. There's absolutely no ulterior motive on his part, he just feels it's his mission to seek answers to his questions. End of story.

After all is said and done, he's the one responsible for the accounting of his life, and sometimes he's made to feel that notwithstanding some utterly brilliant achievements by humans, we're not as advanced as we think and say we are, and his conclusion is based primarily on the observation that those of us who refuse to reason seemingly don't want others to either.

They seem afraid of what they might discover, forgetting in the process that everything around them is as a result of thoughts. Sometimes he gets frustrated to even broach the subject, although he knows he must.

He'd always say, "Thought is the forerunner of action," and he feels like he has to demonstrate that in whatever way he can every time. Furthermore, he doesn't believe there should be boundaries where thinking is concerned. People should be able to think freely, "unfettered," he'd insist, and as justification, he'd say, "Nobody by himself is a repository of all knowledge." What's more, he knows without any fear of contradiction, that nobody, absolutely nobody, in this whole wide world has a monopoly on knowledge, and as was alluded to before, he knows that everything starts with thinking, and so he doubles down on the idea of freedom of thought.

Although he'd hoped that his exploration and embrace of the religious lifestyle would be a game changer, he found out that for him, it wasn't, it was just a flirtation instead. Nothing more! He'd heard, read, and seen so many terrible deeds done in the name of religion and, sad to say, that had the effect of making him conclude that something didn't add up. Something wasn't right! He saw religion's ugly side too often, and it scared him immensely. Simply saying that he was surprised to find that instead of being comforting, it was frightening is one of the biggest understatements he'd ever confronted, given the negative impact such a discovery had on his life. It was devastating! What is also concerning is the idea that man's hardships are as a result of sin. He figures if that's the case, then he must have sinned more than anyone else because pain and suffering are constants in his life. They just won't go away, no matter the means and the times he tried. What's even more puzzling is the fact that for a while, he'd lived an ascetic life, hoping to find that bond with religion, but at the end of the experience, he was as unfulfilled as he ever was. Something was still missing. The message and the application seem at odds. He was looking for unity and certainty, not conjectures and/or wishful thinking. His spirit was deflated; he wanted rational, practical, believable, and achievable goals coupled with good accounting and projections. That's what he wanted, plain and simple.

Despite his misgivings, relief sometimes came in strange ways, and as was said before, no matter how fleeting, it was a welcome respite to his normal way of life. It was therapeutic, so during one of his religious introspections, he recalled hearing the story of a guy who was studying to become a priest but found Latin to be a formidable stumbling block. Well, years later as luck, or ill-luck would have it, one of the would-be-priest's former friends saw and recognized him having a good time at a party.

"Hi, padre," he introduced himself. "Long time no see. Remember me? Trevor, Trevor Feelwell."

"Yes, yes, of course I remember you," he says with a smile. "You were one of my best friends," he said, looking him over. "How could I forget you? How are you?"

"Fine, just fine," he replied with a wide grin. That was his way of setting the tone for what he hoped would be a light and comfortable conversation. "I couldn't help but notice you on the dance floor, padre. You got some moves!"

"Thank you," he replied, and they both laughed heartily.

"Where did you learn to dance like that?" Trevor asked admiringly.

"At the seminary I suppose," he answered himself while the would-be-priest kept on smiling.

"Maybe I need to be a padre, too, if your dancing is anything to go by. Must be a happy place, huh?"

"Well… well, ahem, ah…" he clears his throat. "You see…um, um s…sorry to disappoint you, but…but I'm not a padre…"

"Pa… Pardon me, what did you just say? I didn't hear you clearly."

"I said I…I… I'm no…not a padre," he said weakly, almost inaudibly.

"What are you talking about, stop fooling around, will you? Please stop talking nonsense. This is no time to be fooling around, this is serious time. Don't you think you're taking the modesty stance a bit too far? I mean," he laughs, "it's me, Trevor, you're talking to. We go back a long way. You can be straight with me, you know that."

"I…I guess," he says with uncertainty.

"You…you say you're not a…wait a minute." He pauses, takes a hard look at the would-be-priest and bursts out laughing. "I believe I see what you're up to, following instructions, eh? Eh? Eh?" He pokes him in the side. "You devil you!" he says. "I understand, believe me! I can see it clearly now, yes, sir. They must have told you to highlight the trait of modesty, as someone in the mold of a saintly person would, heh, heh, heh. Good job! You guys are crafty, slick, I mean really slick, and you almost pulled it off, too. I almost believed you, padre. Pardon me, but damn, y'all are good actors, ha! Ha! Ha!"

"No! no! that's not it at all," he says seriously. "I swear. It's like this, I dropped out of the program shortly after enrolling."

"You dropped out?" he asked, expressing shock. "No, I'm sorry, but I don't believe you, no way. One of the things people mostly admire about you, and by the way, that includes me as well, is that you're not a quitter!"

"Well, I …I hate to say it or to disappoint you, but this time I am."

"But why?"

"As…as you well know, Latin is one of the requirements…"

"So?"

"So as far as I was concerned, I found the jingle a friend had taught me more appealing."

"The jingle?" he said frowning. "What jingle?"

"Well, whenever he had Latin class, he'd say, 'Latin is a dead language, as dead as dead can be, it has killed the ancient Romans and now it's killing me,' and that's how I felt, too. I wasn't ready to die yet, not from Latin or anything else, not if I could help it. Yeah! Strange as it probably sounds to you, that's the reason I opted out and…and let me also say that the jingle became so popular that almost everyone recited it." He said that with the conviction of someone who fervently believed that was consolation enough for the decision he'd made to drop out of his studies.

"Well, what's done is done, but I'm so sorry to hear that you, of all people, became a part of the 'almost everyone' crowd and quit. I… I do remember, I can remember well how you used to like to mimic priests by staging mock sermons."

The would-be priest stroked his chin, threw back his head, and laughed uncomfortably, remembering.

"Well, I wish you the best going forward," the former friend Feelwell said, "and it's nice seeing you again. It's been my pleasure, really. Take care. Bye now."

"Bye," he replied, and they went their separate ways.

That aside I.M. became more anxious for answers as he thinks about the limited time he has left on the planet, and nothing that he's experienced or witnessed so far provided him with the level of satisfaction he envisaged or seeks. Not religion! Not atheism! Not even science! Not anything. Nothing provided him with a clear-cut answer, the kind he craves, but he knows it has to be somewhere out there in the mix. The question is where? He also knows he still has a lot of challenges ahead, but as daunting as the exercise promises to be, he'd already made up his mind to continue the search. When things got sticky, he used to remind his friend Rollin that where living is concerned, he was accustomed to the go around part of it, but not so much with the merry part. This latter part he says is elusive and seems to be playing hide and seek with him, so much so that he developed what he refers to as a "why bother attitude" at times, however, it never lasted. Events and time convinced him that that kind of feeling was a luxury he couldn't afford. He just knew he had to get back to and stay in the game, and fast, too. The clock keeps ticking unrelentingly. Tick, tock, tick, tock, it never stops and it sounded ominous, like a direct message to him to do whatever he had to do now before time ran out on him.

3

The Meeting, Part I

But as he contemplates his next move, he heard his doorbell ring in rapid succession, one ring, two rings, three rings, and even a fourth. Gosh, he thought, this ringer must have something important to say and must be in a hurry, too. So insistent!

"Coming! Who is it?" he asked.

"C. Deathe," the person on the other side replied.

He was sure he didn't recognize the voice, nor did he recognize the person he was looking at as he peered through the peephole in his door.

"I'm sorry, who are you again?" he asks.

"C. Deathe," he repeats, "and I'm just your friendly neighborhood salesman with a product I'm taking the liberty to tell you you'll be needing, maybe sooner than you think."

"Wait a minute, don't you think that's a bit presumptuous? I don't know you, and you don't know me, so how can you presume to know what I'll need? Go away," he said fuming.

"Sir," he pleads, "please hear me out. I really didn't mean to offend you, and I'm sorry if I did. It's just that my enthusiasm got the better of me, sorry. Please, please, please let me in and I'll explain what it is that I'm offering in a more detailed and appropriate manner. You could be missing out on something big here, and I know you wouldn't want that, right?"

"I… I guess not. All right," he said, stifling a yawn as he lets him in.

"Thank you." He smiles, extends an arm, and said, "Hi, I'm C-Deathe, and the C is for Certain."

"And I'm I.M. Everyman. Pleased to meet you. And you did say your name is Certain Death, didn't you?"

"Yes, sir, I did, but it's Deathe with an e at the end, D-E-A-T-H-E."

"Oh I see! Thank you for the clarification and also for the comment you made about my name being all-inclusive. That's what I call being clever." He looks him over and says, "Now what can I do for you?"

"Well, let me see." He strokes his chin, pauses, and says, "Nothing, would you believe it, nothing! Strange as it sounds, nothing at all. Well, Mr. Everyman, to put it another way, all I need is your cooperation. That's the size of it. I really want you as my next victim, and I do badly."

"As, as your what? Did I hear right?"

"Sorry," he laughs. "I mean client, can't you take a joke?"

"Excuse me, but I want to know the type of business you're engaged in before we proceed any further," he says seriously. "Didn't you say you have a product to sell or at least introduce to me?"

"Yes, I did, didn't I? A…a slight slip of the tongue. No big deal. You know how these things go. What I really meant to say is that we have a service to offer, a service! We're in the service business. That's what our business is built on." Looking around he asks, "No family members?"

"No, not at the moment. I'm single if you must know, but let's back up to where you said you were offering a product and then you switched to offering a service, which?" Deathe stalls, he didn't answer immediately.

"See, see, you seem to be avoiding my question," he says in an accusatory manner. "Yeah, you're so evasive, and I'm beginning to wonder why." He pulls his hand away from Death's tight grip, grimacing as he does so.

"Oh, no, not at all. Nothing could be further from the truth, I'm not avoiding anything or even trying to, I'll get to that shortly. As a matter of fact, I'll be glad to, but all you need to know at this juncture is that I'm here for you." He curtsies and smiles disarmingly as he says this, after which he hesitates and scratches his head before saying, "You know what, Mr. Everyman, I've changed my mind."

"About what?" he asks.

"About telling you what we offer. You see we always try to please our clients, and since there's a strong possibility that you'll be one, let me be as clear as it's possible to be, in order to avoid any misunderstandings now or in the future."

"I appreciate that," Everyman says.

"I'm glad you do, and to get back to the point I was about to make, it's really quite simple, they're one and the same. The product is the service! I am Deathe," he asserts, "and I don't lie. I don't need to," he continued with a cockiness that is unnerving. "Deathe's my name and nature, sir, and I'm completely at your service." He salutes. "C. Deathe reporting for duty, sir."

"I've heard a thing or two about you, Mr. Deathe, and…"

"Oh," he said, taken aback. "Pleasant things I hope."

"Well, for the most part, but I also heard some very disturbing things as well."

"Pay no attention to that," he says dismissively. "It's just what extremely jealous people do, tear down successful people. Crazy world, huh? We…we," he laughs, "we have more important issues to discuss."

"Such as?"

"You probably won't believe this, but we've been thinking about you so much that we've worked on a plan just for you before the big event!"

"Big event? You've lost me completely. What big event? It sounds ominous, the way you say it."

"No!" he says hastily, trying to allay his fears. "It's not. It's actually what we call 'a get to know you better' gathering between our clients and/or prospective clients and us."

"But I'm not your client," he protested, "neither did I make a promise I'd be! What is the matter with you, eh?"

"Nothing's the matter with me, and don't you worry about it, you'll soon be," he said assuredly. "And remember, whatever you do, please don't fight me on this."

"And why not?" he asked testily.

"Because many have tried before, and you know what…"

"What?" he asked eagerly.

"They all shared the same fate!"

"And what fate is that exactly, if you don't mind my asking?"

"I don't mind, but let this be a warning. They all failed miserably. Is that what you want, too?"

"No! Heavens, no!"

"Good, I didn't think so. Furthermore, you know what it's like to have a relative or a friend missing, eh, Mr. Everyman?" he asked in an unmistakably intimidating manner.

"Yes, sir, I do," he answers nervously.

"I'm sure you do, and I know there's always the temptation to try to defy the odds, but I'm here to tell you in the strongest possible terms that you'll be on the losing end if you try. Shucks… I'm sorry. What's the matter with me? Here I go, predicting outcomes again. Dammit! Well, Mr. Everyman, you've waited long enough, so let me give you a profile of our company. We're…"

"Please do," he interrupts. "I couldn't help but notice the emphasis you placed on the 'our company' description…why is that?"

"Ooo, I'm busted," he said in jest. "And I couldn't help but notice that you seem to object to any and everything I say or do. I don't for a minute think I gave you the impression that this was a one person or even a small operation, but if I did, I'm so sorry. Please allow me to set the record straight. We've always been a big company. We couldn't be otherwise, not with the volume of business we do. We started out big from day one and ya, we've gotten bigger, much bigger, so big you'd never believe." He laughs. "I couldn't run it by myself, never have and never will. It's a very huge operation, and as I go along, hopefully you'll get a better understanding of who we are and what we do."

"I hope so, too, but right now, I'm confused."

"Of course you are, and that's what I'm here for…to clear up any confusion, to…to make the picture clearer. It's my obligation to, so let me say this right now, we're a global entity. Yes, Everyman, that's what we are. I can see the shock and surprise on your face, but yeah, it's true, our operation spans the entire globe. We're literally every-where, and we're harvesters. That's what we do. Reapers, some call us, and we have a very high success rate that's never been duplicated by any other company in our line of work, or in any field as far as we know, and we're damn proud of it. As you know, in any business, especially one as large as ours, we do have our share of mishaps from time to time, but thank heavens, they're minor and rare, and we always bounce back stronger," he crows. "So far this year, the harvest isn't as good as for the same period last year, but there's no reason to panic as our projections for the rest of the year show us exceeding our target by a wide margin, and I do mean wide. Yippee, the level of profitability will be unprecedented. Added to that, we pride ourselves in being truly equal opportunity reapers. As a matter of fact, we're pioneers as far as that feature is concerned. We…we conceptualized and implemented its use, and we can say so without any fear of contradiction. And yes, we're proud to say we do not discriminate in any way whatsoever. We do not even use the D word anymore. No, sir, that's not in our vocabulary anymore. It's gone! And it shows how serious we are. If you doubt me, and I hasten to say I see no reason why you should, you can ask around, or better yet, go to our website, SureThing.com."

"My, my, my, that name speaks to confidence. Are you really that confident?"

"Weren't you listening to me about our projections, etcetera?" he asked annoyed. "We don't joke about such matters," he adds. His frustration was evident; he sighs and says, "Oh, what's the use."

"What was that?"

"Oh, you didn't hear?"

"No!"

"It's just as well, and if you'll let me, I was about to say we think it's very appropriate considering…" His voice trails off as I.M. interjected.

"Considering what?"

"The competition, the demands we have to fulfill, the job we do, and last but not least, the result we get from doing it. That, my friend, one learns to appreciate, and we do. We're very proud of our brand," he adds, patting him vigorously on the back. "Very proud! This is a seminal moment for us. We…we wanted something that said dependability, and by golly, that's the image we portray according to the more respected rating agencies. Just think about that…we're satisfied we did, and so are they. Nobody," he emphasized, "and I do mean nobody has to worry about age, race, color, size, weight, creed, religion, politics, or anything of the sort. Oh, what a beautiful thing. Except for good service, there's no exclusivity here, we take them all. Rich or poor, we take them all. We cater to everybody. It's what's referred to as truly 'world class' service. I mean, there's no other business like ours on the planet, except for birth maybe. In this business, we say, 'If you come, in time you will go.' I say that to say we're just stating facts, and I'm assuming that's what you want to hear. Am I right, Mr. Everyman?"

"Oh, yes, yes, I most certainly do."

"Well, if that's the case, here's more; we're a twenty-four hours a day, seven days a week, 365 days a year operation, and we also work that extra day on leap years, too. This is no job for the weary or the faint of heart, if you get my drift. Talk about a business that's customer friendly and you're talking about us. Sure thing, thank you very much."

"And how long did you say you're in business?"

"I don't recall saying, but if you must know, ever since creation."

"My, my, my, that long, eh," he said in awe.

"Yes! That long, and we love it. We absolutely do and wouldn't change it for anything else in the world. We're a dedicated bunch, and it's as people often say about the jobs they love."

"And what do they say, Mr. Deathe?"

"It's heaven sent," he answered without hesitation, "and I'm very pleased to inform you that we have a new business plan, a plan which is entirely contingent on how you behave."

"Are you calling my behavior into question, is that what you're doing?"

"No! All I'm saying is how you behave can nullify or enhance your chance of being on the plan, it's in your hands, that's all I'm saying."

"So what's this 'new' plan all about?"

"It's a plan whereby you get a big discount if you come along willingly."

"Wha…what does that mean exactly?" he asks stammering.

"It simply means that if you co-operate fully and not resist our overtures, and/or if you introduce our services to relatives and/or friends, you'll be eligible for the afore-mentioned discount. Additionally, there's also this pay before you go plan that's in an advanced stage of development and could be enacted anytime now. I'm giving you a heads up, so please use the information wisely." He chuckles. "We're very anticipatory you know, Everyman, and we're proud to be recognized as a forward-looking entity, and by the way, did I mention that we've drafted and submitted a resolution on the matter, and we're confident of its approval by the Board real soon? What we're proposing is way ahead of whatever our competitors are offering. Smart, eh!" he said, raising and lowering his eyebrows. "Think about this…"

"Think about what?" he asked baffled.

"We have so many good plans in the works, and they're all geared toward benefitting our clients, and I don't know if you've heard, but we've even earned a new name if you follow the latest news in the 'trade papers.'"

"What name? What do they call you, your company I mean, what, what?" he asked anxiously.

"The Innovators Squared!"

"Well, I've heard all you've said, but let me tell you this, Mr. Deathe or whatever the hell your name is, I'm not interested in you or your damn company, and I sure as hell won't be introducing your services to any of my friends or relatives. Copy that!" He was seething with rage and panting as he talked. "Further…furthermore, I'm not going anywhere anytime soon, so don't hold your breath waiting," he said bristling. "Let me say this again, Deathe, loud and clear, if you're soliciting my help, forget it! It ain't gonna happen, that's my message to you!"

"Mr. Everyman, Mr. Everyman, calm down please. There's absolutely no reason for you to be carrying on like that. All I'm doing is apprising you about our company and offering some reasonable propositions in the process. Your behavior makes me wonder if you've taken leave of your senses, have you?"

"What's that supposed to mean? The answer is no, no, and no. I'm as rational as the next guy!"

"So, so if that's the case, can I call you I.M?"

"What did you call me just now?" he asked, his tone softening.

"I said I.M. Did I say something wrong? Any objections? To the best of my recollection, I think I may have called you that before."

"No!" he answered, "you can call me whatever you want, that won't change my mind," he added resolutely.

"Oooooweee, somebody sure is testy today, anyway, suit yourself, but know this, by not taking me up on my offer, you stand to lose substantially."

"By the way, how did you know that's what my parents called me?"

"I didn't, that's just plain coincidence, that's all that was, and as for the offer I made, it's the way to go, and I mean that literally. If you stand by your decision, I do believe you'll live to regret it. I couch it in those terms because I don't want to shock you, and that's all I'm saying on the matter. As people say, you have the 'last word,' Pappy. He laughs. One last thing, being the democratic person that I am, I respect your decision, however, I must tell you I'm disappointed by it and wish that you'll reconsider. In fact I'd recommend that you do."

"Reconsider, ha, there's nothing to reconsider. My mind is made up. The matter is closed! Or let me say it in a more amiable manner, please consider the matter closed, however, as I said before, you can call me I.M. Those are my initials after all. I'm comfortable with them and I don't see or foresee any harm in that, however, I'm doubtful about us ever being friends."

"Oh, please, get over it. I'm sure that in due time we'll be, and once more, I applaud you for your honesty, however, I think you need to be reminded that one never knows for sure how events and/or relationships will turn out. We may yet become friends, not just friends but bosom friends."

I.M. squirms.

Deathe laughs, clears his throat, and says, "I'd like to take a selfie with you if that's ok with you."

He gives him the ok sign as he pulls up closer, "I don't mind."

"Well, I.M., my reluctant friend, I hope that this selfie situation will serve as a reminder that today you looked Deathe straight in the face. My question is do you understand what that means?"

"Yes, sir, whatever," he says vacuously.

"Whatever! What kind of an answer is that? My advice to you is not to say that you do if you don't. Does that make sense to you?"

"I suppose."

"This is serious business, and the last thing we want is to have an impasse with our clients, sorry, or prospective clients, plus there's also this other thing I ought to tell you about…"

"What other thing?" he asks impatiently. "You're talking in riddles again," he admonishes.

"I'm sorry that you feel that way, however, I think that you should know that ours is a very large family scattered by the exigencies of the service we provide. We're all over, and we do anything and everything to satisfy our clientele," he says proudly. "I'm saying this to let you know that you shouldn't be afraid to ask us for any favor, please, please, please don't be. Always bear that in mind. It's one of our strong suits. Oh, oh," he continues as he puts a hand to his forehead. "I'd intended to have my favorite niece accompany me on this visit, but she had to be elsewhere. She's learning the business from the top you know. Lucky girl!"

"Isn't or shouldn't it be the other way around?'

"What do you mean?"

"As I understand it, most people learn from the bottom and work their way to the top."

"That's not what I meant. I'm saying she's learning from me, and I'm the top dog in our organization, that's all I'm saying. Anyway, she loves it very much, just like her uncle. That's what we live for, and she also likes to tag along with me. You could say we have a special bond."

"So why isn't she here since as you say she loves working with you so much?"

"Oh, that!"

"Yes, that!"

"Because she was committed to a previous engagement and I don't mind, she deserves the break, and as a bonus, she'll be able to socialize with her peers. Our off-the-charts overall growth over the years demanded a celebratory party, and we couldn't think of anyone better to represent us, hence her absence."

"I see."

"You do?"

He nods.

"Good! What I need to talk to you about next is my follow-up visit."

"Your follow-up visit," he repeats, twitching.

"Yes, that's right. I'm taking the liberty to assume you'll invite me back, and if you do," he said excitedly. "I'll be accompanied by my lovely niece, the one, the only Premature, that's my promise. She's single, smart, very successful, and a sight to behold. She's the talk of the town, and maybe together we'll be able to convince you to move away from here."

"Move!" he said surprised. "Where to if you'll excuse my asking?"

"To a better place naturally," he answers excitedly.

"And where is that?"

"To a place of rest," he says, "and in my humble opinion I think you deserve that."

"Does the place have a name?" I.M. grills him.

"Sure," he answers clearly, then dramatically lowers his voice to a whisper as he names the place.

"I can't hear you, say it louder please."

"I said Undergrounders Retreat! Did you hear me?"

"Yes, but I've never heard of it."

"I didn't think so, otherwise you'd have been there already or just itching to get there as fast as you can."

"Have you ever been there, Mr. Deathe?"

"Why do you ask?"

"I prefer firsthand knowledge, and since you're the one telling me about it, I think it's reasonable to assume you've been there."

"And I don't think you want to delve into whether I've been there or not. What's important is that we make it possible for you and others to go there, but since you asked, yes, I've taken countless others there many times and now it's your turn. What's more, when they go there, they get so attached to their new home, they never leave.'

"Is that right?"

"Yeah! Where have you been, and who have you been talking to? It's like a dream world, a paradise, and that's the kind of place I want to take you to. You deserve no less. Besides going there myself, all the reports I've been having from others about it have been positive, and so I can't understand why you'd want to hesitate by asking this, this barrage of questions. The question that comes to my mind is why wouldn't you want to move to paradise? Everybody else wants to. Beats me."

"And you say the place is as advertised, it's not just what you hear but also what you've seen based on your many trips there, huh?"

"Correct, and it's also very reassuring to note that relatives and close friends of those who reside there say, and I quote, 'They're in a good place.' Seems to me that's as good a testimonial as one can reasonably expect. They're pleased by all accounts. Come on now. Besides, when you get there, you won't have to wonder anymore. The good news is you'll have first-hand knowledge, and soon hopefully."

"Geez! It really sounds wonderful the way you tell it."

"Well, even with all I've said, you haven't even heard anything yet."

"Are you kidding me, there's more?" he asks feverishly.

"I hear that even the planners of the facility are beside themselves with pride and joy when they hear other people describe their creation as 'magical.' They, meaning people, a lot of people, say everything about the place makes for a out-of-this-world feeling, and from what I know about the place, the names of the streets and the layout are things one only dreams of. And this is a dream that is now a reality. Lucky you!"

"Oh, yeah! It sounds like my kind of place," he says, barely able to contain his excitement.

"You bet it is, and as much as I'd like to, it's too extensive a subject for me to tell in just one sitting, however, here's a hint; the main square is called Promiseland Square, and some of the main streets are Heavens Pathway, Street of Gold Boulevard, and Dreamers Paradise Avenue, among others. My best advice would be to get there, and get there fast, my friend." He glances at his watch. "I'm about to wrap up here as I think you've been provided with adequate information about our company, its policies, and some of our key personnel, however, I feel as if I'd be short- changing you if I didn't remind you what the popular sentiment about the place is…"

"Yeah, please remind me, Mr. Deathe. What is it?"

"I know I've probably said it already, but I feel it deserves repeating. They say it makes them feel 'out of this world,' and those comments are solely from the visitors. Imagine what the residents would say and what it's like for them, especially remembering that none of them have tried to leave. Makes the stories we hear about paradise believable. I must also tell you, before I forget..."

"Before you forget what, Mr. Deathe?" he interrupts.

"What was I about to say, oh, oh," he says after a brief pause. "The place is becoming so popular and desirable that only relatively few places will be reserved, and it's been confirmed you're one of the lucky qualifiers. Congrats!"

"Why is that, Mr. Deathe?"

"Why is what, Mr. Everyman?"

"Why do they say it's out of this world?"

"I dunno! Maybe it's the way they feel as the talk going around suggests."

"What talk?"

"My, my, my, haven't you heard? The talk is that to them, the visitors, it's like that utopian place they often hear and dream of. The place they're longing to be...heaven!"

"Did I hear you correctly when you said that your niece, Ms. Premature Deathe, will be accompanying you on your next visit pending my say so?" he asked, abruptly changing the subject. "Is that what you said, sir?"

"Yes, that's correct. You heard right. Do you know her?

"No! I don't know her. That is to say we've never met."

"Well..," he hesitates sensing a mood change. "Ah, ah, is something the matter?"

"Why do you ask?"

"Because you seem a bit unsettled. Is that resentment I sense?"

"I dunno, it could be, although you speak so glowingly about her."

"I'd appreciate it if you'd stop dancing around the question and be specific. I'm anxious to hear what's on your mind."

He clears his throat and says with disgust, "I've heard of her shenanigans."

"Her shenanigans! What shenanigans? What exactly are you saying?" he asks infuriated.

"Seriously?"

"Yes, seriously," he replied without flinching.

"Well, let me see, the list is so long, I don't know where to start."

"List, what list? Humor me."

"Are you sure you want to hear?"

"Yes! I'm sure. Maybe you don't have anything on her as I suspect you don't."

"We'll see, mister adoring uncle, we'll see. Word on the streets is that she's a menace to society, she's a maniac, and she's ruthless, totally."

"Come on now. People can say anything, but that doesn't make it true. Is that all you got?"

"Heck no!" he says. "That's just a start. I've got lots more!"

"You do?" he asked surprised.

"This is the latest story making the rounds about her," he proceeds to say, and as a way of preparing for it, Certain scratches his head, leans forward, and anxiously awaits the unfolding of the story while pondering what could be so incriminating.

"Multiple sources say she's earned the reputation she has," I.M. continued, "mainly because of her heartlessness, and it is worthy of note that these aren't just multiple sources, but for the most part, highly respected and reliable news organizations, and I'm calling for your attention to that particular aspect just in case you have any misgivings about the reporting."

"I… I have a lot but please continue."

"One of the sources swore on his mama's grave that what he saw was astonishing and beyond belief. He said he saw sweet lil' miss Premature walking by a partially open casket containing a body that was there for a viewing in another two hours or so at the dearly departed's former place of worship and …"

"So…what's unusual about that? That's normal activity if you ask me," he says irritated.

"That's what I'd have thought, too, but for the fact that nobody else was in the chapel at the time, except for her and a few select members of the death squad."

"The what squad?" he asks.

"Sorry to be so blunt. To put it another way, I mean your and her close family members. They're the ones the people on the streets refer to as the 'death squad.' My understanding is that Premature was in charge and her assignment was to see that the event went off smoothly."

"I'm sorry, but I still haven't heard what you're so worked up about. I mean, what's incriminating about that?"

"Just keep listening, that's all you gotta do. I'm told that as she walked by, she heard a muffled sound emanating from the coffin, went closer to investigate the source of the sound, and heard a weak but distinct cry for help, and to her further surprise, the body seemed to come to life and was struggling to raise itself to an upright position."

"Well, well, well, the story's starting to get real interesting, what else?"

"I told you. I told you it would," he said with a flourish, "and hear this, it was said that a shocked Premature wondered aloud if she was the witness to a miracle, or was this some sort of a prank on the deceased's part. She wasn't sure which, but she sure as hell wasn't taking any chances. She was heard to say, 'Wha…what the hell is this? What you trying to pull, eh? Come on now.' She'd somehow expected an answer, and you could tell by the way she positioned her ear near the coffin, anyway, she didn't wait for it, she continued talking, doing so while pushing him down in the coffin and eventually closing the opening. 'What you doing, punk? Where you going? Sure looks like you didn't get the memo,' she laughed, hideously. 'Doc pronounced you dead, and I happen to agree with him 100 percent.' She puts her ear on the coffin and says to the deceased, 'Come on, say it with me, if it's good for doc, it's good enough for me, too.' After that episode, she pats the coffin with her hand and said, 'Thank you, you slime ball. You're dead meat and you're gonna stay dead, mister low life. I don't usually curse the dead, but I'm making an exception where you're concerned. How could I not? Wha…what you tried to do is despicable, even by your standard. You tried and almost succeeded in embarrassing our company, and me in particular. That, mister man, is inexcusable, and there are consequences, and as for you walking out of here, I don't think so. You'll be carried out of here as planned. You damn sure won't be walking outta here. Not on my watch. Bye, hope you enjoy the other side.'

It is noteworthy that such ugly and glaring incidents have caused some people to say that this generation of Deaths/Deathes seem to lack even basic ethical standards. They say they're out of control and should be reigned in and cite frequency of occurrences like this, and the display of callousness as the main reasons for their outrage. I hear they're even trying to figure out a way to boycott the firm and have gone to great lengths, even to hiring 'experts' to find a solution, but so far the 'experts' or anybody else can't think of anything that's workable, and until they do, it's the same story — death rules!

Talking this and talking that, Uncle Deathe was getting tired of hearing I.M. berate his niece and his organization. He was sick of it and maybe at another place, at another time, it would have developed into a brawl, but this time he exhibited a level of self-control that not even he knew he had.

"Gee whiz," he said, looking at his watch, "just look at the time, where did it go? Please say you'll forgive me!"

"For what? What should I forgive you for?"

"I'm late for another appointment, and I simply have to go. Truth is I enjoyed your company so much, I overstayed," he laughs.

"You sure that's what it was?"

"Yeah, I'm sure, and by the way, let me also commend you for your conversational skills. It's formidable. I was engrossed the whole time, although I take umbrage with the unfair portrayal of my niece. She'll be vindicated, mark my words. I'm confident she will, and you wanna know why…?"

"Why?"

"She's innocent, and innocence will win the day!"

"Maybe I should call her Miss Innocent, huh?"

"Maybe you should because that she is!"

"What a name," he laughs.

"What name?"

"Innocent Deathe, ha-ha."

"Have your fun, but remember what they say about the one who 'laughs last.'" He extends an arm and says, "It was my pleasure meeting you, Mr. Everyman, it truly is, and we'll be back to see you soon hopefully. Here's my card- C. Deathe, Heaven's Doorway. That's all the address you need. Bye now, and thanks again for the selfie." He smiled and walked out the door waving.

SONNET ON IGNORANCE

Down in the valley of darkest despair
Locked in ignorance's magnet-like prison
A place where ghosts fear to enter
Life became a series of sullen-faced Everests
But alas! My hopes gleamed
Like fingers of light
As resolved I am
To conquer man's nemesis
O slumbering mind awake from thy rest
Stop taking abstractions for reality and reality for abstractions
Let solutions course to and fro' on thy pavements
Transforming ignorance to knowledge at my behest

Reflections

There are moments when no matter how depressed you are, someone or something lifts you out of it, and the contrast couldn't be more stark than the recent visit of Certain Deathe and the recollection he has of a celebrated and widely respected sportscaster of yesteryear. The story goes that at the presentation ceremony, in awarding the trophy to the owner/coach of the winning sports team, TEAM CAN DO, the sportscaster with head held high, a gleam in his eyes, and a glow of satisfaction etched on his face walked briskly and proudly to where the coach was standing and said, "Ladies and gentlemen and others…" immediately the crowd bursts into laughter, not letting him finish whatever else he was about to say.

"Ladies and gentlemen and others," he said again amidst the laughter, "good evening, make some noise… er, er, please give it up for coach Foot and his team, TEAM CAN DOOOO." The applause was quick and deafening, interspersed with some doggie-style sounds, "Huru, huru." After the cheers had subsided somewhat, he offered his personal congratulations to the team, then he turned to the coach and said exuberantly, "And how are the little Feet doing?" referring to his two young children. Raucous laughter erupted almost immediately the question left his mouth. The sound from the microphone had carried throughout the venue and beyond, yet strange as it seemed, he wasn't offended by the laughter. The thing is he'd learned in English class way back when that the plural of foot is feet and good student that he was, as far as he knew, he was just speaking proper English.

Say what you want, he's a traditionalist and darn proud of it, too, so when the laughter got even louder, he beamed and was heard congratulating himself with words to the effect, "Good job, boy! I can smell promotion in the air! Did you hear the laughter and the cheers, good job, oweeee." He felt as if he was at the top of his game and nobody could tell him differently.

As a result of all the things that I.M. had seen and heard, he concluded that the only certainty in life is uncertainty. Nobody knows for sure what's going to happen from one moment to the next. And with the woes he's had and continues to have in his personal life, he often wondered how that "stretched out arm" referred to in the scriptures never seem to extend far enough to reach him. Another observation that he considers instructive is that man seems to be the only animal wanting or capable of caring about his origin or his future, and as far as he knows, the only species that keep records and make projections about life. Given such facts, he's mystified by people who expect to hear stories with happy endings only. His own experience taught him that's not how the world works. Life is not a fairy tale for most. It's real and so are the outcomes, sometimes happy, sometimes sad, and as was mentioned before, as for his personal life, he's more familiar with the latter.

Confusion reigns, for example, when one looks at the religious and the evolutionist divide, each side says it's right, so the question is how can things which are diametrically opposed be both right? Such theories invite polemics, and why should something so important be the object of speculation, mere guesswork? There are myriad areas of confusion, and he wants the veil lifted in his lifetime. A prime example of what he finds strange is the Adam and Eve story. How could they produce offsprings of different races, colors, etcetera? Did they get help, and if so, who from? Another mystery is how could people live so long in biblical times, even to hundreds of years, yet in this age when medical science is much more advanced, nobody comes close to living that long. Why isn't that replicated today? Still another thing to contemplate is why is faith so important since it is said that without works it is nothing, and the companion question is why bother to work if the only way to salvation is by GOD'S grace? Another question that comes to mind is if sin is man's nemesis, why was it introduced, as it is said that GOD is all-knowing and therefore knew what the outcome would be or is it, as some say, the most convenient way to explain needless pain and suffering, especially knowing that as regular people it is impossible not to "sin." And by the way, who made Satan and why?

Could Noah's ark stretch, and if no, how could it carry so many animals, some of them wild, dangerous, and extremely large among other things? Additionally, there are a host of questionable things about this story, for example, if man with his supposed superior intelligence can be so disagreeable, are the storytellers saying that the animals behaved better, given their temperament and proximity, etcetera?

Questions, questions, and even more questions. How come "bad" things happen so often, even when you don't want them to, but for the goods things to happen, there are a lot of conditionalities, such as don't stop praying, be patient, and be believing, etcetera, how come? Nobody has to pray or wait patiently for the bad things to happen, they just happen, and often too, too often, how come?

When you pray, and if you're like most people who never had their prayers answered, there are the apologists, and it may sound harsh to describe them that way, but they're always suggesting that you probably didn't pray "right" or HE'S "testing" your faith. It's really strange and only serves to widen the credibility gap, and as if that's not enough, I.M.'s worried that his call for clarity will be construed by some as him putting GOD on trial.

Maybe they need to be reminded that GOD said to prove HIM.

Is he wrong for not wanting to stumble his way through life or to feel that there should be a blueprint that's understandable, believable, and achievable, is he? For a very significant part of his life, he's been battered, bruised, and trampled upon, yet he still keeps clinging stubbornly to life. There's that deep-down feeling that something's missing, that lingering and haunting sense of un-fulfillment which makes him wonder what's next.

Some say he must be nuts, others say delusional, and they all wondered aloud asking what dreams could he have left to fulfill even while admitting he was still relatively young. They made fun at the thought saying the only practical thing for him to do is to give up. He's only wasting time, precious time at that. Some even went as far as to say that wasting time was like a job to him and that they just couldn't think of him achieving anything of significance now or even in the future. That door was closed forever they say. After all, they reminded, they're talking about I.M. Everyman, and everybody knows he's a serial failure. The blunt truth is he'd failed at almost everything he touched, jobs, relationships, and so on. They reminded one another that after he won the poetry contest, they thought he'd move on to loftier heights for certain, but it'd seem as if that other fellow Smutty Mutty was right all along, I.M. didn't have what it takes. They started to say he had the "unmidas" touch, and they racked their brains in vain as they couldn't think of anything left for him to fail at. To them he was the personification of failure and they conveyed to anyone who'd listen that the only distinguishing feature about him was his ability to fail. They belabored the point saying that when it comes to failing, he was a legend; he was very successful at it, so when the question was asked amongst themselves, what else was there for him to fail at, the place went silent.

They were dumbstruck, and it took some time before someone shouted unkindly, "The only thing left for him to do now is die, and given his history, he'd probably fail at that, too," or as someone else suggested, "He'd be one of the remnants the scriptures talk about." They all broke out in laughter and chanted, "remnant, remnant."

Nobody had to tell them, they knew what they voiced were outrageous, preposterous even, but because he'd failed at so many conventional things, they ran out of rational ideas and substituted the unusual out of sheer frustration. That was their explanation.

In the past, whenever he felt unbearably burdened, he'd get down on his knees and pray for help as per the guidelines of the scriptures and preaches alike, but he'd noticed that instead of relief, things got even worse, and this was another addition to the frightfully long list of religious shockers handed to him. He just couldn't believe it, and he didn't know what else to do or where else to turn. Besides that, whenever he complained, he was told again and again what he'd been hearing all his life, be faithful, don't stop praying, the LORD works mysteriously and no one, no not one would be burdened beyond his/her capacity to endure etcetera, etcetera. What! What! For him such exhortations and teachings were the breeding ground for frustration, and so his confusion grew to extraordinary proportions and it led him to conclude that unless and until he died under the weight of his burden and unless it was before their very eyes, too, there'd be no other way for the "select" to be satisfied that he'd indeed gotten more than he/she could withstand. This made him wonder if the preachers and others of that ilk were lawyers posing as preachers; they were that evasive, and on the rare occasions they weren't, they suggested that he probably took things "out of context." Their words. This in turn prompted him to ask, how could prove HIM and just believe be taken out of context? What an idea! He thought about it for a while and dismissed the suggestion, concluding that such directives were too explicit to be misinterpreted. What it did was make him more aware of the fact that these were the same people who'd constantly told him that everything is possible as long as he believes and prayerfully takes it to HIM the most high GOD. They'd also told him that empirical evidence support such claims, but the "WORD" by itself is good enough, so there's no need for worry or doubt. Notwithstanding such claims and encouragement, all he got for his efforts were grief and more grief, grief without end, and so it was not surprising that he morphed into a skeptic.

And in the midst of all this chaotic situation, he remembered a chance encounter he had with Rollin who'd become a very good friend and confidant over the years. They exchanged greetings as friends do, after which I.M. said, "with knowledge comes power, right?"

"I believe that's akin to what they say, "Rollin agreed and they both laugh cheerfully.

"And what is also true," I.M continued, "is that there are multiple ways of arriving at the same result, right?"

"Yeah, I suppose," Rollin said thoughtfully. "Where are you going with this?

"Fair enough, I'll explain. Let's take the number four for example…"

"Well, what about the number four?" Rollin interjected.

"I believe that you'll agree that there are infinite ways to get that number mathematically, or any other number for that matter, for example: 2x2; 2+2; 6-2; 16 /4, and so on. What that suggests to me is that with thought and application people can get the same result using different methods and that should not only be a lesson to us all, but should also lead to better understanding among peoples. Sometimes," he continued, "we get wrapped up into our own 'little,' world and we tend to forget that we're creatures of our respective environments, and so we behave according to how we've been socialized. Well, so does the other guy. I just thought that was a common sense thing because if we switched environments, they'd behave like us and we'd behave like them."

"That's exactly right! I think your analysis is brilliant except for the fact that you seem to be overlooking one very crucial element."

"And what…what is that?" he asked, lost.

"That common sense ain't so common," he said smiling.

"Rollin', Rollin'," he said in admiration. "You nailed it! So simple, yet so profound." It's as if he had an epiphany.

"That's so on point. I just never heard it explained like that before. Good job, and that's another reason why I enjoy talking to you, young man." They smiled, after which I.M. said, "Well, my friend, since I have you in the here and now, and before we say our until we meet again, there's this burning question I'd like to ask."

"Oh, oh, here it comes. Sounds serious."

"It is. Have you noticed how people who seek tolerance the most are themselves the least tolerant?"

"Have I ever," he answers. "It's as they say, their way, and yes, you've got it, or their way." Afterwards they hugged, patted each other on the back, and went their separate ways.

This "home at last/home sweet home refrain" doesn't provide him with any respite, as by himself he's always thinking. The absence of family means he's alone with his thoughts and they come at him with alarming speed and frequency. Sleep is the only relief he gets, and he wants everybody to know that his desire to find out his purpose for being here and about his future after passing, is not an intent to vilify any person, religion, or it's beliefs and practices. He wants that to be clearly understood as he has no hidden agenda whatsoever, but whenever he thinks of his pending passing, it raises questions which in instances challenge and conflict with the philosophies he was taught about such matters. Furthermore, he believes fantasy supplants reality often-times and he wants to know whether it was by design or was it coincidence. He further feels that the fact that he has to question the motive makes it suspect. What he wants is reality, not fairy tales, and he's not sure what he's getting.

He calls it his "here and now" and his "there and then" purpose. To be candid, he's downright conflicted with the competing claims of creation versus evolution, the chicken and egg situation yet again. On the one hand, creation seems impossible, given the Adam and Eve version, and evolution takes so long no one in his own lifetime can honestly claim to see the changes, yet for all the mystery these conflicting theories pose, man is here!

That's undeniable and beyond dispute, man is indeed here, and as Rollin would say, "That's an inescapable fact!" We see evolution in architecture, art, music, even life styles, etcetera but not in the physical transformation of humans. What evidence we have would seem to suggest that we've looked the same for thousands of years, and our reliance is mostly based on scientific evidence involving long and arduous studies, which by the way are still in progress, thus incomplete and by extension, inconclusive.

To compound matters even more, and despite the on-going efforts, all we have are assumptions about the methods used in building the pyramids of ancient Egypt or in the attempts to explain the mysterious rock formation at Stonehenge, etcetera. This is precisely why he thinks that miracles of the kind as portrayed in biblical stories and times are needed today and could be the much talked about "game changer." In today's world, people are accustomed to seeing magicians do tricks and illusions, and they're presented as just that, tricks and illusions, not miracles, and that notwithstanding the fact that most people who attend such events don't have a clue as to how they're done and so he's resolute when it comes to the idea of miracles because adding to an already complex situation we see not only the emergence of "new GODS" as exemplified by politicians mostly, but we're also reminded that different societies globally have had and in some cases still have their own GODS. It's just confusion everywhere.

There's even strong advocacy by some that GOD is female, and in some societies, there are multiple GODS, such as GOD of water, GOD of fire, and so on. Some of these GODS are not easily replaced by new ones, if ever, and if he recalls correctly, that is what the sociologists refer to as "customs, folkways, and mores, etcetera, etcetera." That's what he's dealing with, and since he's not able to get the answers he regards as satisfactory from any other source so far, conventional or otherwise, he internalizes a lot and finds out that no matter where his thoughts roam, invariably they come back to the haunting issue of what happens next. He also remembers the times when he felt rejected because he was treated like a disposable item, as if his spot could only be on the scrap heap of life. Yes, he suffered hell along the way including many life-altering injuries. Some say he was just at the wrong place at the wrong time while others were just as convinced that it was his destiny, but whatever it was, it just so happened that every time there was a semblance of recovery, some other bad thing happened. In one instance, he'd been accidentally shot in the groin area while leaving a friend's birthday party. In another instance, just days after leaving the hospital from that near-death experience, he was run-over by a hit and run driver who didn't heed the red light, even though I.M. was half-way through the crosswalk. He stopped briefly, surveyed the scene, and took off again as if nothing happened.

In times like these, he wished he could do whatever he was thinking to the driver if he ever caught up with him, and this in turn jolted his memory to the story he'd heard of a guy who was tried and about to be sentenced for attempting to take justice into his own hands, but as he was about to be sentenced, he looked squarely at the judge and said, "Well, your honor, by the same token, attempting to lock me up is the same as locking me up."

That aside and to continue the litany of woes that beset him, he was robbed in broad daylight while taking a stroll in a park, stubbed his toe in a crack on a city sidewalk resulting in a broken hip among other things, and get this, he was never compensated and he was robbed for the second time when he used a short-cut on his way home from one of his usual early morning walks, and this time it was at the point of a gun. Then there's the time he was hired by a singer for his backing band, but when time came for him to perform as a soloist during a recording session, his saxophone squeaked endlessly. He made a quick examination and found that the soap he'd used to plug the holes in his instrument weren't there anymore, and the story goes that at that point he made a frenzied dash for the nearest exit, and to this day it is argued that his feet had to be made of wings as absolutely no one on the planet could catch up with him. They also said his instrument had more holes in it than the target at a shooting range. Stories come and stories go and most of his, or to phrase it better, most of those about him were painful and as such had a dampening effect on him and his faith especially. He doesn't have the faith he once had in religion, life, or anything for that matter. He was truly depressed. They could call him all the names they want, but nobody could accuse him of not trying.

Here's a guy who'd burned the midnight oil, did whatever society asked, no, demanded of him, yet he still hadn't experienced the long hoped for halcyon days. That was society's promise, so where are those days hiding and why? To make matters worse, there's hardly a yesteryear for him to get nostalgic about. That's for other people, not him, and he's scared to even think of tomorrow, and during moments like this, his thoughts wander, and this time he reflects on the idea that even though animals don't read books and stuff like that, for the most part, they seem able to make sensible decisions on their own, in order to survive. He wonders what drives them, and it's not lost on him that they also demonstrate the amazing capacity to learn commands in whatever language they're exposed to. He's captivated by that and thinks it's remarkable, and so he gives thanks to the heavens for reminders like that. Nobody knows better than he does that when things get really dark such reminders help to shore him up. To him they're inspirational and make him wish that the pleasant moments of his yesteryears, however fleeting, would continue into his todays and even carry over into his tomorrows, but that never happened. At such times, it seemed as if that was a line he wasn't supposed to cross, the happiness/success line, and although he came close to giving up at times, he never did. He pretty much willed himself to overcome whatever was preventing him from achieving his goals and even pledged that if and when good fortune came, he wouldn't discount the role that the difficult times played, in-as-much as he hated them. "Challenges," he called them. With that said, his vision of the hereafter is murky. It's uncertain at best and that upsets him considerably. There's no road map to follow, and as such, he can't shake that "what lies ahead" feeling. Despite not having a "road map" however, something is always happening in his life, and while most of the time it may not be what he wants to happen, he mostly devotes time exploring some of the more fundamental tenets of organized religion and notices among other things that even long-established churches increasingly change their postures in order to accommodate the sentiment and practice of the secular world so's to become relevant and popular, and they do so while simultaneously preaching that GOD ALMIGHTY never changes, and he thinks that's dichotomous! The widely held belief that mans' curiosity is limitless is under-scored by his own curiosity as he tries to unearth answers to a wide range of topics including how people who've been cremated and whose ashes were scattered in the wind or the ocean or wherever, be made alive again, and while he welcomes answers from anyone, it's aimed prima-rily at the religious community because they're the ones who con-stantly claim that humans including some who've already transitioned will inhabit the "new" earth.

He also wants to know why was Peter so faithless; remember he couldn't walk on water.

And why was Thomas so disbelieving; remember he doubted the resurrection. Remember also they were both disciples and witnesses to miracles done by JESUS we're told, so how can mere mortals, or better yet "regular" people, mere hearers and readers centuries later be expected to develop such noble traits of faith and belief, especially knowing that some of those who "walked" with HIM, didn't or could-n't, how? Is it far-fetched to think that man will become extinct, given the fact that dinosaurs and a host of other animals have, and as a fol-low-up, maybe the question should be when, considering how reckless our stewardship has been and continues to be. Maybe, just maybe, some people may have a valid point when they say we only live once, which and/or what is true? Sadly, there are those who treat life so cal-lously that he's left to wonder if they even think about the next phase or even care. He, on the other hand, cannot understand that approach, as his own appetite for information about the future is insatiable and he'd give anything to know for sure if people will recognize their loved ones and their pets, or will the past be totally forgotten in line with biblical teachings, which in essence say, "Everything will become new." Once again one has conflicting views coming from the same source, religion!

Furthermore, will there be free will, and if so, won't the same problems we have now arise again, and if not, does it mean that those "selected" will live in a robotic state? Will there be a religious convergence, and if there is, what will it be based on, number of adherents, popularity, doctrine, etcetera, etcetera since each makes the claim that it is the right one, what? Christianity does, so does Judaism, Islam makes a similar claim, Hinduism, Buddhism, and so on. Again, what determines the right one? To him this is confusion plus, or as he sometimes calls it "structured chaos" and that's why "he wants to know what he wants to know" as he says, "while he is and not when he becomes a was." The latter situation is impossible, and he likens this situation to people who sometimes delay important decisions because there's no precedent. What? To his mind, there's always a first time for everything, otherwise no decision on anything would ever have been made, and it concerns him greatly that in this day and age, people could resort to such disingenuous excuses. He calls them "apologists," no matter what they call themselves, and he hopes that his search and research about the hereafter will unearth the kind of researchers that we can repose our confidence in and can be justly proud of.

5

The Unlikelies

As a result of three consecutive best-sellers that I.M. had written, he'd been giving inspirational speeches all over the world for a while, and he finds it stimulating and therapeutic, and the novelty of it all seemingly never wears off because he'd sometimes pinch himself in order to test the reality of the situation. He, I.M., had become successful and famous and a celebrity. Wow! Who'd have thought this possible! What a turnaround! And with all that's going on, it's not lost on him that people who never gave him the time of day before were listening to him with a keenness reserved for heads-of-state and/or other such luminaries, and most of all they seem to value his input and also made it obvious they wanted to make his acquaintance. He'd always secretly longed for a forum in which he could air the causes he'd wanted to spotlight and now he has that opportunity, he says it's a "blessing," and so in giving his talks, he'd always try to keep his philosophizing to the bare minimum and also to be as realistic as possible. Case in point, he never encourages the idea that everybody should strive for leadership positions. He knows that's impossible. Everybody can't be leaders. In reality most people are and will always be followers. What he does instead is to tell people to never let go of hope.

"Hope is the key for everything," he'd say. It's in his view, one of the best, if not the best word in any language. Not only that, it's also one of the best feelings one could ever have. It's aspirational. And talking about best, he'd sometimes tell his audience to learn what the best do and try to out do the best. Another sentiment he stresses often is that you can't win if you think like a loser, and you can't lose if you think like a winner and then he'd say, "Hope is life." Finally, he'd cup his ears in the palm of his hands and say, "The word of the day is...."

And he'd hear a chorus of voices say, "Hope." Most times he'd also exhort his listeners not to look only at results but more importantly why the results are the way they are. To him thoughts are powerful, and he often refers to them as "forerunners to action," but he also knows that some of his own thoughts and conclusions about long held beliefs would be challenged and even ridiculed. He expected that. All he asks is that the discourse be civil, shed light on the topic/s, and that those with opposing views remember they have no more right to think than he does. He feels strongly that if their thoughts and actions were considered safe for society, so should his. He knows that his are considered a paradigm shift from the prescribed conventions, but he feels such conventions are unproven at best and downright confusing and might not even be provable. What he knows for sure is that when it comes to deciding his own future, he hasn't deferred to anyone. It's something he'd want to do himself, so there's absolutely no delegation outside of himself, and that's why he's so engaged with this exercise.

It's not something he takes lightly. It means everything to him, and he wants everyone to respect and understand that responsibility belongs solely to him for as long as he's capable. No capitulation, no genuflection, no obsequiousness. Those traits were never his forte, reasoning was and is, so is his voice, and last but not least, thoughts! He's repulsed by the notion that anyone could or would decide things for him without his knowledge or consent and hopes that never happens, so despite the lack of satisfying answers to the many queries he's made about the after-life, such set-backs tend to spark his enthusiasm for more research, not curb it.

Looking at I.M. and judging how "at home" he looks, it would be an understatement to simply say he enjoyed these get-togethers. He loves them! He lives for them! It's not just a way to inspire and/or get things off his chest, it's also very exciting, so on his way home from his latest "talk" in a popular part of town, he noticed prominently placed signs in bold letters reading, "DEATH RULES, DEATH FOREVER, DEATH IS NEARER THAN YOU THINK, YEAH, YOU ARE ONE STEP CLOSER TO DEATH, HUH HUH," plus the drawing of a dead man's skull under the caption, "A LITTLE PIECE OF DEATH, WELCOME!" He stopped briefly, taking it all in, and at the end of it all, he was furious and his contempt for this kind of reprehensible behavior reached an all-time high.

"Who could've..." he didn't even finish the question as he just couldn't fathom what would prompt anybody to behave in such a deplorable manner.

He calls it "disgusting and depraved." The crassness of it all and the gravity of the situation elicits a barrage of questions from him ranging from "Why? What? How? "Which?" to "Who?"

In earlier times, he'd have no hesitation in putting the blame on Smutty Mutty. It bore his "fingerprints" and it's something he'd be prone to do. Back then he was known as the consummate prankster, but for some time now, a very long time in fact, all that has changed, causing some to say the "new" Smutty Mutty rightly belongs in the turnaround section of life, and not just in the turnaround section but the "dramatic" turnaround section. If you were a betting person during his adolescence, you'd think or say or bet that he was heading straight to jail or someplace like that because of his troublemaking. All the signs were pointing that way, but as the saying goes, "that was then," not now, and that's meant to include even going back years. That's how long he's broken that habit. Some people even go as far as to calling his outcome a "miracle," and it could very well be. Who knows, the change has been that drastic. He's certainly not the Smutty of the past, no! No! No! he's a changed man, and the consensus is that he wouldn't do such a thing, especially not when he's riding the wave of success, popularity, and recognition his career as a master of ceremonies has brought him. He attends popular events, mixes with high profile people constantly and does a lot of radio and television commercials, and is highly sought-after year-round.

Looking back everything started when he "cursed out" I.M. at that award celebration way back when. That was without question the turning point in his life. You could say the "right people" heard him and were impressed, so impressed that they invited him to be the master of ceremony at various events, and as it is said, "What followed is history," and in all of this, he found time to marry his high school sweetheart, Rita Fleetfoot. She lists her profession as homemaker, but she also does a highly profitable online business from home. When asked they constantly remind people how happy they are, and it shows. Besides, they gush with pride and joy when they talk about their children, grandchildren, and the soon-to-be great grand and insist that life couldn't be better.

People generally, and friends particularly, have a tendency to overuse phrases sometimes to describe Rollin Glee and others in his position as very successful, and in his case, they can be forgiven because he is very successful. His admirers, a lot of them, claim he has the "midas" magic and points to his various endeavors. All of them successful.

He's I.M's closest and most faithful and trusted friend, and just to be clear, he was never ever considered at anytime as a candidate for creating the mess that I.M. abhorred so much. It never crossed his mind, and as for his success in life, there was never any doubt he'd be, and he delivered in a big way. He first broke into the limelight as a stand-up comic and later had his own syndicated television show. He became such a sensation that when he performed on the "road," it was to standing room only audiences. His shows were sold out affairs, and his trophy room is filled with numerous awards from all parts of the globe. He's mobbed by admirers and autograph seekers everywhere he goes and have had to resort to numerous disguises in order to "escape" from the crowd at times. Notwithstanding the fact that he's a very busy man, he contributes time and money to numerous charities at home and abroad and says that aspect of his life is most "fulfilling" and "like a dream come true." When asked about his marital status, he says that although he came close to doing so several times, he somehow just never got around to doing it, and although he's not superstitious, he felt as though there was a message there, and that's all he'd say on that particular subject, except to say he's "happy."

Because of their successes, and despite their "tight" schedules, they were for the most part moving in the same social circles, so it was not surprising that on occasions they came face to face with each other at events and not only talked about current happenings and future plans but also "old times." Whatever animosity there was was long gone, and they talked and laughed about any and everything as though it was like that all along.

"Guys, guys," I.M. said when they had a chance to be by themselves, "I have a few things I'd like to share with you and probably get your opinion on before we leave, but first I'll tell you a very short story about a past neighbor and me. Want to hear it?"

"Yeah, let's hear it," they all said.

"Well," he began, "we had a difference of opinion on a matter we were debating, so during a very short pause in the conversation, he used the time to point to his dog and said, 'See why I don't want any other friends besides my dog?'"

"No, I don't," I said. "That's crazy! Why is that?"

"Because he never talks back," he said pointedly. They laughed, after which I.M. said, "But you guys can talk back to me if you want to." More laughter followed after, and when it subsided, he continued with the conversation, "All right, now that everybody's in a good mood, isn't it true to say that we break with tradition whenever we think it no longer serves us adequately, isn't that what we do?"

"Yeah!" they all agreed.

"So why should it be different with 'certain practices?'" he asked.

"I suppose by 'certain practices' you mean religious among other things, huh?" Rollin asked.

"Yes, that's correct," I.M. said, "but let's stick with the religious for a moment."

"It could be for a multiplicity of reasons," volunteers Rollin.

"Such as?" I.M. pursues

"Fear of the authorities/status quo and because of customs," Rita said.

"And the backlash from public opinion and so on," added Smutty.

"You know what, I think you're all right, but I also think that y'all recall that in ancient times people who had certain diseases were stoned out of existence in instances because nobody understood the nature of the diseases or had a cure or even knew they were diseases. Some even went as far as to label the inflicted as being cursed or demon possessed and used that as justification for their injurious and sometimes fatal reactions and as was alluded to, mostly out of fear and ignorance. Is this what we want today? I know I don't, but I'm not gonna force my beliefs on anybody. Everybody has to make up his own mind. Before I let the subject go though, I'd like to give just one example of what I'm talking about, and remember there are countless like examples I could use as support for my viewpoint. I want you to visualize how we travel today as compared to how it was done, let's say 200 years ago, and tell me which would you prefer. You know what, I'll leave it at that as the answer speaks for itself, and that is why I think some customs warrant change. I rest my case."

"That may be so," says Rita, "but how do you explain the prediction, or as some people call it, the prophecy that in the last days people would be fleeing oppression and doing so with little or no compassion from anyone, especially seeing that these so-called prophecies were made ages ago?"

"That's a very good question, Rita, and I hope my answer satisfies y'all. It's my belief that historians worldwide documented such happenings over the years whenever they occurred, plus there were a handful of other people who were branded as being 'ahead of their time' who were able to foresee such things, so viewed in that light, it's not as mysterious as it sounds. There was a clear pattern to follow."

"There's also a lot of false accusations and suppression of the truth lumped under prophesies, too; what about them?" Smutty said.

"Again, this is nothing new. It's been going on for ages, and the only difference to my mind is that it gets reported on more often and by more people simply because of how 'news' is reported today."

"Well, what about the wars and rumors of wars?" Rollin asked. "The famines and the frequency and damage of natural disasters?" he added.

"As for the wars and rumors of and the famines, they were always there, only underreported, and where natural disasters are concerned, it's the same thing, ahem," he clears his throat, "there's also an added dimension, fear, and a predisposition to view such occurrences as GODLY events. In addition there's the environmental aspect as some people build and live where they're not supposed to and are polluters to boot, etcetera. Well, if there are no more questions, I just wanna say thank y'all for a spirited and enlightened discussion, even if we disagree at times. The good news is that we came in as friends and we're parting as friends! Bye, y'all, see you later."

The Meeting, Part 2

Back at home, he was so engrossed with the recent meeting he had with his long time friends that he didn't hear the chimes of his door-bell ding-dong, ding-dong, and when he snapped out of his trance-like state, he asked, "Who is it?" His heart pounds loudly and rapidly in his chest.

"Why don't you guess," a voice cheerfully came back at him.

"Look, Mr. Whomever you are, I don't want to be rude, but I'm a busy man and I don't have time for games with strangers or anyone else right now. In other words, I don't have time to waste, understood?"

"You sure don't," he giggles. "That's for sure."

"What did you say, and do I even know you?"

"As a matter of fact, yes, you do know me."

"Did I make myself clear? I'm very busy."

"Aw, come on now. Be a good sport and open up. Remember me, I'm Deathe, Certain Deathe. I'm sure you remember me from our last meeting. I...I just thought you'd recognize the voice, that's all."

"Recognize the voice," I.M. repeats while trying to figure out who the owner could be. He didn't feel like getting up from his seat to peer through the peephole this time. He was exhausted and didn't want to be bothered.

"Yes, as I recall, we did have an extensive conversation a while back and we agreed there'd be a follow-up visit in the very near future. Don't you remember?" He didn't wait for an answer, he just kept on talking. "Well, Mr. Everyman, this is it, that follow-up visit that we talked about. There's unfinished business we need to discuss, and as promised, there's someone I'm anxious for you to meet."

"You don't say."

"Yes, I do say."

"All right, I'll open the door and let you in," he said resignedly.

They shook hands briefly but vigorously, and for the second time in as many visits, Deathe had a firm grip, and for the second time, I.M. had to pull his hand away. Deathe chuckles, after which he introduced his niece, saying, "Mr. Everyman, ah, ah, I.M., my friend, this is my niece, the lovely Premature."

"Pleased to meet you at last," Everyman said smiling.

"Likewise," she replied.

"Your reputation precedes you."

"Oh," she said surprised. "And just so you know, I've heard so many good things about you, too; so much so that I feel as if I've known you forever and so I feel very comfortable in your presence."

"Thank you, and the sentiment is mutual," he says giggling.

"I'm glad you feel that way. Er, can I ask you a personal question even though we just met and all?"

"I…I…I guess so," he said uncertainly, "yeah, yes, sure, go ahead," he said with certainty this time. "What is it, what is the question you want to ask me, young lady?"

"Mr…er…er," she began clumsily.

"Pardon me," he said uneasily as he saw her struggling and assumed it was his name she'd forgotten, "you can call me I.M. if that makes it easier for you to remember. I won't mind."

"I.M…I.M." she mulls over the initials. "That's so sweet. I.M. Everyman," she smiles.

"Yeah! You got it. That's the name of the beast," he jokes.

She smiles in a beguiling manner and says, "Oh, stop it! You don't look anything like a beast to me, quite the contrary."

"Thank you," he replied blushing but with a big grin on his face, too. "You're too kind, heh, heh."

"I…I remember your name alright," she says, "maybe too well."

"Come again," he invited.

"Come again?" she asked frowning.

"Exactly what do you mean by that, missy?" he asked in an aggressive manner.

She hesitated, "Well, the question I have to ask is…"

"Go ahead," he encouraged, interrupting her midway through her question.

"Is…isn't it true to say that…that you lost one of your best buddies recently, Mr. Everyman?"

"Yes, that's correct if you're referring to the late great Mr. Always Around. Such a tragic loss, too. I can hardly believe he's not with us anymore or the stories I've been hearing about his passing, and I hope the perpetrator/s will be caught and held accountable to the full extent of the law." He sniffles. "I'm more than willing to put up a reward for the capture of the barbarian/s for such a dastardly act."

"Dastardly, you say, what did you hear?"

"Sorry," he replied. "I just can't get into that right now, maybe later."

"You seem quite passionate about it," she said testily.

"Yes, I am…very."

"Well, if it's any comfort to you, so am I, and I'm deeply sorry for your loss."

"Thank you! Did you know him, Ms. Deathe?"

"Yes! I'm afraid so. I'm the one that took him out, if you get my drift."

"You what? You did what?" His mood changed drastically and abruptly. Whereas it was lukewarm at first, it got downright hostile. It's as if she'd touched a raw nerve. "I'm asking you again, and I'm expecting straight answers. You did what? To be more specific, I'm asking what do you mean when you said you took him out. That's the language of gangsters, are you, eh?"

"Oh, no, I'm not. Don't get me wrong," she stammered. "I simply meant to say I was the one that took care of him," she continued awkwardly.

"You did, huh? You're kidding me? And so damn brazen about it, too. So…so you admit to killing my friend, huh?'

"No, no, no, and no!" she protested. "Not so fast! No way! I didn't kill anybody. What I'm saying is that I was the one who supervised the event after his casket was brought to the church for viewing, and if it means anything to you at all, I made sure he was put away properly."

"Look, sweetheart," Certain Deathe chimed in as coolly as someone who'd been exposed to situations such as this before would. "You don't have to be nervous or defensive about anything, honey. You did nothing wrong. He's just clutching at straws. He's got nothing on you.

Deep down in his heart, I do believe that I.M., excuse me, Mr. Everyman knows that you did your best, and the record will show that you did as the job demanded. In fact you did more, not less, and I'm glad that you were the one that presided over the event. Good job! I'm very proud of you, in fact the entire organization is. Everyone is, or nearly everyone is talking about how excellently you and your crew performed. GOD!" He makes the sign of the cross, "Thank you, we're so blessed to have the likes of you as part of our work-force." He follows this up by looking to the heavens and saying, "Lord knows we could use more people like you. You're the consummate professional, salute!" Turning to I.M., he says, "I recall that in our very first meeting I stressed how caring, affectionate, and efficient you are dear, didn't I, I.M.?" They exchange winks while I.M. had his eyes glued to the floor. "Didn't I, I.M.?" he asked again, louder this time and more insistent, "I said, didn't I?"

The meeting wasn't going as planned. From the very beginning, it had gotten off to a rocky start and that hasn't changed. I.M. was in shock and utterly disgusted by what he'd heard from the pair and what he calls their "clumsy" effort to hide her murderous deed. It rattled him to his core. How could anyone be so repugnant, he thought to himself, how?

The slimy mother.....ers, and as he cursed, it brought out an overwhelming and sudden urge to spit in both their faces, and that was a temptation he found very difficult to resist, yet he managed to somehow, and to Deathes' relief, "Yes," I.M. answered at length.

"As I told you on our way over, I said only nice things about you, dear. After all what else could anybody truthfully say about you. Your record is impeccable. It's as everybody knows, the envy of the profession, and I don't for a minute think that someone, someone as informed, as intelligent as Mr. Everyman would be inclined to carelessly throw his lot in with gossip mongers against principled members of society, especially seeing that he's at the forefront of the movement for Principles in Society. I'm taking the liberty to say he wouldn't. Would you, Mr. Everyman?" He was so hot with anger, he didn't answer right away, instead he pretended he didn't hear the question. Deathe seized on the non-response and said, "I didn't think so," then he turns to his niece and says, "Sweetheart, I love you and I think you're very special."

"Geez, Uncle, thank you. I'm very appreciative of your support, and I'm so pleased to tell you the feeling's mutual. After all is said and done, you are the one who groomed me. I learned from the best. Thanks again," she said curtsying.

At this point, I.M. found it extremely hard to contain himself from getting into some form of physical altercation with them, but every time he attempts to do something rash, something else, something much stronger keeps telling him to be calm and so he looks from one to the other and thinks, "sickos," too good a term to describe them both, maybe the "evil twins" would be more fitting. And the thought did cross his mind that this could be the perfect time to puke all over them as he feels nothing would be more appropriate for the pair of them.

"Everyman," Deathe interrupts his thoughts.

"Yes, Mr. Deathe," he says respectfully while smiling broadly. "What is it this time?"

"I see you've got a big smile on your face, what…what's going on?"

He smiles still and says, "Nothing really. Just a thought, ha-ha-ha."

"Mind sharing it with me?"

"No, it doesn't really concern you," he lies. "Nothing you'd be interested in."

"Really? You seem a little tense to me, almost as if you're hiding something, and you called me Mr. Deathe."

"Well, isn't that your name?"

"Yeah, but why the freaking formality? I thought we'd moved beyond that stage a long time ago. You need to relax, or as some would say, 'chill,' and just in case you haven't noticed, smile, you're in Deathe's territory or soon will be." He said all of that, looking as if he was ready to pounce.

"And here I am thinking I was in my own home. Please excuse me for thinking so," he says in mockery.

"Didn't I tell you to relax just now. You're too uptight and combative, like…like a stick of dynamite ready to explode. How many times do I have to tell you that I see you as nothing more than another victim, eh, how many times, I.M?"

"You see me as what?" he questions alarmed.

"Holy crap," he cradles his head in his hands, "what am I saying. Must be the beers I had on my way over. I'm so, so sorry. I mean I see you as a friend or at least getting close to being one. Sorry."

I.M. groans, then asks, "How close is close?"

"Closer than a brother," he replied, smiling and composed again.

"That close, eh? Well, let me warn you, I'm not of that bent," he says unexpectedly.

"Of what bent? What are we talking about now?"

"I'm heterosexual if you must know."

Deathe laughs good-naturedly, "Well, so am I," he says, "and oh, no, that's not what I meant at all, and to be honest, we couldn't care less. You must not be familiar with our slogan, it says, 'We take them all,' and we do." It's more than a slogan you know, it's policy." Notwithstanding his seemingly good-natured laughter, he was thinking more serious thoughts about I.M., this "no-good bastard," as he often refers to him. That "joker," another of the names he calls him, doesn't know how many times he'd come close to getting a foot up his ass, the son of a b...ch. What's prevented that from happening so far is the fact that he wants I.M's full confidence before he "takes him down."

"One of the things that intrigues me about you, Mr. Deathe, is that you have no reservation telling me you're a man of principle and how you'd go to any length to uphold the law, so my question to you is how come you breach the notice on my door, which clearly states in bold letters. BY APPOINTMENT ONLY. How come, huh?"

"Notice on your door," he says sarcastically. "Are you serious?" He was about to go ballistic; he got up from where he was sitting, paced the floor, then decides it would be wiser to strike a more conciliatory tone, and so he playfully slaps I.M. on the back and says, "What's up, dude? Lighten up! What's really going on in that head of yours?" He didn't wait for a reply, he just kept on talking. "We can and should do something about this contentiousness that's been creeping into our discussions, don't you agree?" He didn't answer but appeared to be deep in thought. Deathe meanwhile turns to his niece and says with a half-hearted smile on his face, "See what I have to go through with this guy, honey?"

Little did he know that such a simple question would spark a new round of hostility as no sooner than it left his lips, I.M. shot back.

"Well, can you blame me? Ever since we first met, you've been issuing nothing but veiled threats at best and I'm here to tell you I'm sick of it! Furthermore this is private properly, meaning this is my home and off-limits to whomever I say, including you! You just can't come up in here whenever you please. This has to stop, you hear me? Who are you? Better still who the hell do you think you are, Deathe?" He ponders for a little while, then said, "You know what…"

"What…what?"

"I think I may have a solution," he said animated. "Yes, sir, I do!"

"What are you talking about, and what solution? Solution to what?"

"I…I think I'll move," he blurted out.

"Excuse me, did I hear you right when you said you're thinking about moving to another location? Is that what you said, Everyman?" his disgust building.

"That's right, Deathe, you heard right, and by saying what I did, I knew I'd get your attention. What you gonna do about that, Deathe?" he taunts. "Wait, don't answer that, just know that I'm gonna move, so your sorry ass won't be able to bother me anymore, and I sure as hell won't leave a forwarding address or anything like that. That's what you call off-limits. Finally, Deathe, at last, Deathe, a bastard like you won't be able to get to me. How's that for a plan, eh? Ha-ha-ha," he laughs.

"Well, Mr. Everyman…uh-uh I mean I.M., sir, you're a smart man," he says, toying with him. "First of all, I was about to explode when you talked about moving and so on."

"But why would you be so mad?" he asked rhetorically. He didn't mean to, but before he was able to stop himself, the question had already popped out of his mouth.

Deathe seized on the opportunity to chide him and to gloat.

He rolls his eyes and says, "Because you'd be upsetting me, or to put it another way, you'd literally be taking the food out of my mouth so to speak and we can't have that, Everyman, we just can't. That's a no-no. Besides it's kinda hard tracking down people once they decide to live the nomadic lifestyle. You know as well as I do that it takes a lot of resources and a lot of time, however, what do you know, ta-da, we have a system so to do."

"I…I don't understand," he said mystified.

"Don't worry, you will in time, and second of all, all I can tell you again is we have our ways. As I just said, a system," and he said that with the calm of someone who's sure of himself. Someone who leaves no doubt that he knows what he's talking about, and that scares I.M. It makes him jittery and leaves him sulking. "Furthermore," Deathe continued, "didn't I tell you we're a worldwide organization with a worldwide reach, eh, Everyman, didn't I?" he scolded. "You see when you talked about having a plan, I said to myself, wait a minute, he's got a plan, we got one, too. So sorry, you're not the only one with a plan, buddy," he informs, smiling triumphantly. Everyman winced. "Let me break it down for you, we're everywhere!" he says with emphasis. "There's absolutely nowhere in this world that you could move to without us knowing. You can't hide from us, son," he teases. "Sooner or later we'd find you, ha-ha-ha-ha." He nudges him, "How's that for coverage, eh, how's that? Ha-ha-ha-ha. We've got you covered, Pappy."

I.M. cringes. If what this guy's telling him is true, there's no safe haven anywhere. In effect he's trapped.

"Let me get this straight, so you're fuming about me coming to your home unannounced, right?"

"Right!"

"Well, I didn't, that never happened, but even if I did, so what!"

"So what!" he repeats heatedly. "Is that all you gotta say?"

"Yeah, let me let you in on a little secret. No amount of notice and/or security can keep me or any member of team Deathe out! Do you understand me," he said irate. "Do I make myself clear, Everyman, and by the way, have you taken care of your business yet? You've been advised to time and time again. Have you, Everyman?"

"What business are you talking about, Deathe?" he asked incensed and followed up by adding sternly, "my business should be of no concern to you, you're damn impertinent. It's just as it says, my business!"

"You ask what business am I talking about…look here, don't play dumb with me, Everyman," he warned. "Ok, smart ass, I'll tell you, or rather ask you. Did you make a will yet, eh, did you?"

"A will," he repeats flabbergasted.

"Yes, a will-power of attorney, that sort of thing. And get this, you're hearing it straight from the horse's mouth," he chuckles, "or in this case, straight from Deathe's mouth. It doesn't get any more real. You so remind me of the guy who said he was 'unprepared for his unpreparedness.' If I were you, and I'm glad I'm not, I wouldn't hesitate, no, sir, not even for a second and please, whatever you do…" He falls to his knees in dramatic fashion and continues pleading, "please, please, please don't let me have to leave you for other agencies to handle your situation. Frankly, I wouldn't wish that for my worst enemy. Don't get me wrong, there are a few upstanding ones out there, but unless you know them, you'll get the dregs. They're plentiful."

"Gentlemen, gentlemen, please calm down," Premature, who was mostly listening, decided to break her silence and chimed in. "Let's bring back some semblance of civility to our discourse. I know we can, so let's do this. Come on now," she urges.

"Well, forgive me for asking," I.M. said cautiously, "but last time your uncle and I spoke on the health of your company, he said there was a downturn in the business, so what's the situation now?"

"Thanks for your interest, that's a start, and I'm glad that you asked. Please also remember to keep us in your prayers. After all it's people like you we're depending on to help us grow the business. Thanks again for your interest, and to answer it directly, as of now I'm happy to report that business is thriving. There's absolutely no other way to describe it," she adds giggling. "With that being said, please allow my uncle to bring you up to speed, uncle, please," she beckons.

"Well," he responds laughing, "there's even an increase in animal deaths if you're interested in that kind of statistics, only difference is that animal rights groups provide some sort of protection for animals, especially those they consider to be on the so-called endangered list, but funny enough that sort of vigilance doesn't extend to humans. That's really funny," he laughs uproariously. "That...that's so sad, a real pity," he said, still laughing.

"What do you mean when you say, and I quote, it's 'a real pity?'"

"As I said," and he bursts out laughing again, "there's...there's no like protection for humans. Makes you wonder, doesn't it? Ha-ha-ha-ha." He laughs uncontrollably for an unusually long time before saying that he has to wonder if the animals were the ones making the rules. "Seem to me," he says, "humans are the more endangered of the two," and he goes into that jeering laughter again.

"What a mess! I guess the silver lining in all of this is we're happy, extremely so!"

"Who is we, and why are you so happy?'

"Don't you mean who are we, and isn't it obvious?"

"You know exactly what I mean, or could this be your way of avoiding the question?"

He rubs his palms together gleefully, and with a big toothy grin on his face as is his habit when things are going well, he says, "It goes without saying that by 'we,' I mean people in our line of work generally and our own company particularly. What that means is that we can expand our business/es. What is also of great significance to us, Everyman, is that it shows that our analysis is perfect. Kudos to our team, especially our planning department, and our clients of course. Can you believe that the exact same topics we highlighted and discussed at our last board meeting including, I might add, the results we aimed for have been realized! That's just incredible. It's a joy to see things falling into place as hoped, I tell you. It's such a wonderful feeling, so fulfilling, and I'm extremely happy to share such an extraordinary experience." He was on a roll and there was no stopping him. "Yes, he said enthused, "it's great to know that our company is on such a sound footing, and even better if that's possible, considering that our investors are extremely happy. In a word, elated! We fully intend to keep the momentum going, and I hope I can interest you, Mr. Everyman…"

"Interest me in what, Mr. Deathe?" he asked surprised by the invitation itself and its suddenness but also flattered. "What…what exactly should I be interested in?" he pressed. "You've lost me completely."

"Listen up, man, I was about to invite you to our grand celebratory party and…"

"You're kidding me, right?" he asked in a more subdued manner, his emotions mixed. He felt honored and suspicious at the same time, and in the excitement, he said, When?'

"Soon!" he replied. "The date is tentative as of now," he said lying, "but to be brutally frank, I have my reservations about you."

"Re-re-reservations about me, why is that? I have my reservations about you, too."

"Oh," he laughs. "I don't mean it the way you think. It's just that something deep inside tells me you may not be around for it. Such a pity as I'm sure you'd enjoy yourself, tut, tut, tut, damn it!'

"Why did you say I'll probably not be around? That's so frightening."

"Probably! Is that what I said? Oops."

"Probably or may not, what's the difference?"

"Well, to that, all I can say is, I must be slipping big time. I should have said you won't be around. There, I've said it, satisfied now?"

"Hell no! What do you mean, and why? What is it that you know that I don't?" He was visibly shaken and angry and the questions came tumbling out one after another. "Why Deathe? Besides you, who else Deathe? Who else? Answer me! Now!"

"Everyman," he replied, "don't for a minute think that I don't see what you're doing, and I must say you're damn good at it, congratulations! My guess is that you've been taking acting lessons somewhere and your tutors must be real proud of you, I know I am. Let me also say this, although the temptation is great, I repeat, it is great and I'm impressed, but I'm not gonna go there with you. Sorry, I'm just not doing it. No, sir! No thanks!" He shakes his head from side to side, "I'm not falling for it. I'm not falling for your bait. No way! I want you to know that my resolve is strong." He laughs. "Everyman, Everyman, Everyman, mmuhh, mmuhhh, muuhhh, you're good, but I'll have you know that before coming here, I'd just led and left a bible study group and our topic, believe it or not, was temptation and how to effectively deal with it. So there!"

"Excuse me, gentlemen," Premature said as a way of letting them know she was ready to rejoin the conversation. She directed her gaze to Everyman and said, "To your earlier observation regarding what you referred to as our 'unusual' first names, you're right, but some of us do have 'regular' names, too, you know."

"Such as?"

"John, Mary, etc. Our names speak to our characteristics mostly. Let's say Instant were assigned to you, there definitely wouldn't be a second visit; there'd be no follow-ups. Absolutely none. If the task wasn't immediate, he wouldn't accept the assignment."

"I see."

"Yes! The names are reflective of the personalities that go with them," she continued. "I will confess, however, that the more familiar names, such as the Johns and Marys, are designed especially for the person next door effect."

"Aha! So…so you agree that deception is not only rampant but is also encouraged and tolerated in your operation, huh?"

"No! Not at all." She was emphatic in her denial. "I'm not confessing to anything. That's not what I'm saying and you know it. No way! Shame on you! Just because we're a near-monopoly doesn't mean we don't strategize. Who doesn't? We have to. These days one has to use all kinds of creative marketing tools or go under, and for your information, we have no intention of going under." She sighs. "And…

and let me state it for the record, your surprise attack has not gone un-noticed. It was scurrilous, malicious, and utterly uncalled for. Shame on you, Mr. Everyman. Frankly, after such an ambush, I don't know how you can live with yourself! That's how rumors start and that's how they spread! And may I say, you're one lucky bastard… sorry, ma…ma…man."

"Why…why do you say that?"

"Say what?" she asked heatedly.

"That I'm a lucky man?"

"Because it's true," she answered in a more measured tone, "and as I hear it, correct me if I'm wrong, this is my uncle's second visit, and that can mean only one thing!"

"What does that mean? I'm almost afraid to ask."

"Well, don't be! He likes you, and for whatever reason, he must have taken a very special liking to you. Most of us don't do second visits as I explained before. Congratulations! And please remember this, we're a proud and close-knit family. In addition we're proud of our heritage, our name, and especially our work ethic. We're second to none in that regard, and we support each other fiercely. That's who we are and that's what we do," she brags.

Deathe's eyes lit up as he nods his head in agreement, claps his hands together and says, "Yeah, that's how we roll. Talk about profes-sionals and you're talking about us, baby. We not only make the claim that's also our game, meaning whatever we say we do, we do. A lot of people hate us, or so it's claimed, but sooner or later, they come to the realization that they can't escape us, oh, oh," he covers his mouth and says, "I meant to say avoid us. You paint pictures with words as a poet and/or inspirational speaker does and we sing songs of thanks-giving whenever we're able to 'win over' people as yourself." He leans toward his niece and whispers, "I can't wait to take the son of a b….h out and litter some landscape somewhere with his sorry a…s," after which he says loudly for I.M. to hear "she's a good ambassador for our company, my friend." He smiles, adding, "She's the best, yes, sir, the very best, and I wish I could invent a language filled with only superlatives just for her. That's how good she is and what she means to me. She's a blessing, and we as a company are very lucky to have her." Turning to her, he says, "Young lady, I'm so very proud of you. I adore you, and know this, the company does, too, so a big thank you from all of us. Big up! You deserve it, and as I've said so often, we're lucky to have you. That can't be overstated."

She in turn smiles and hugs him as she expresses her gratitude.

Turning to I.M., Certain said, "Everyman, our actions are irreversible, and yes, you heard right, and that's why we have to be so careful in our undertakings. What we bring to the table is professionalism. In a word, trust. We've never lost sight of that! Everyman, um, um, Mr. Everyman…um, um, I.M., as I said before, this is strictly a business call, not a social call, so no hard feelings and as such…" He never finished whatever he was about to say as I.M. interrupted again.

"Exactly what are you trying to tell me Mr. Deathe, and how long will you be around this time?"

"To answer your last question first, I'd say for as long as life lasts."

"That long, eh?"

"Yes, I'm afraid so, but if the signs are right and everything works out accordingly, it shouldn't be a long wait, and as to what I was trying to say, it's simply this: we've never lost anyone before…"

Again I.M. interrupts, "My oh my, that's an impressive record anyone would be proud of. Keep it up!"

"That is our intention, and that's why we don't plan on losing you either."

"Me?" he asks, alarmed, and that triggers a series of loud moans from him. "Losing me!" he repeats.

"Yes! You!" Certain laughs. "Long live death," the Deathes chant in unison.

"No need to worry though, I.M.," Deathe continues. "You know influential people, although I hear that the welcoming committee can't wait to meet and beat you, oops, meet and greet you. Gosh, please forgive me, I mix up words sometimes, plus all this excitement gets me all tongue-tied, anyway, as you already know, we're here to escort you to your new abode, as we understand it, your final destination."

"Final destination, new home," he says exasperated. "I...I don't want to go anywhere with you guys," he protested.

"Sorry, bud, but I'm afraid that's not up to you to decide," Deathe said matter-of-factly. "The time has come and that time is now. Don't be mad at us, please," he mocks. "We have to follow protocol, and I'm sure you understand such customs being the man you were, sorry, I mean are. We're...we're just doing our jobs, no hard feelings. By the way, do you know what bothers me the most about you, Mr. Everyman?"

"No, I can't say that I do."

He stomps a foot and says, "The haunting knowledge that I was foolish enough to introduce the likes of you to my sweet, lovely, innocent niece. The award-winning, up and coming rising star of our company, the acclaimed toast of the industry and soon-to-be face of the industry, and the best you can do is offer doubts and insults concerning her character and achievements." He puts a hand to his fore-head and said, "What was I thinking! Let me start by saying that's low, even for you!"

"And you let me stop you right there, mister," he says, ready for a fight. "This sad situation didn't arise because of my imagina-tion, or as you would say, my 'machinations,' or idle speculation. Let me remind you that there are numerous news reports that dis-seminated those stories about your niece and your entire organiza-tion. These stories are widely circulated by the media, a plethora of media outlets I might add. In other words, the full gamut. In ad-dition you, yes, you, and you can stop pointing at yourself as if you're surprised. I can assure you that won't change the facts. And don't even think about asking me if I mean you because I do. You have wittingly or unwittingly corroborated at least some of those same stories in your own recitation of events to me. So the question is, why blame me, and what's your motive?"

"So you're telling me that you believe the gossip mongers despite the fact that I've gone to great lengths to assure you that they're false-hoods, plain and simple. They're nothing but fabrications. That's all they are, fake news and more fake news!"

"Well…"

"Well, what?" he presses.

"They sound real to me, and from what I've gathered, a host of other people, too, enough people to make you uncomfortable," he argues.

"Am I to understand that what you're telling me, Mr. Everyman, is that you believe the stories and news outlets that specialize in rumor mongering over me, is that what you're saying?"

He clears his throat and says, "It's annoying that you keep asking the same question over and over, Mr. Deathe, when it's common knowledge, and even you can't deny the extraordinary lengths some of you, in fact most of you will go to in order to achieve your goals in your industry. Besides, there's tons of additional information out there designed to apprise us on what to watch out for, so…so let me get this straight, are you saying we should not heed these warnings, we should ignore them instead, is that what you're saying, Mr. Deathe?"

"No! Not at all. That's your right and obligation, and I respect that. All I'm saying is that I can speak unequivocally for our company and tell you we do not, repeat, we do not condone such practices as you've described. We've never ever made such unsavory moves, never, not even once in our long history in the business. Quite the contrary, and I'm seriously beginning to wonder when or if the blindfold will ever be lifted from your eyes. When are you going to understand what those monsters, yeah, that's right, that's what I call them, monsters, and I make no apology for doing so. When will you understand what they're capable of, eh? We don't do such things, no, sir, not for a minute, and we're definitely for enlightenment. As you well know, we're at the forefront of that drive, and not to boast or anything of the sort, but we've contributed generously to the cause over the years, so…"

I.M. squirmed and shifted uneasily.

Deathe notices and says, "What's the matter, Mr. Everyman, you want to say something, or are you having a seizure or something?"

"No! No! No! none of them, thank you. I'm ok, and you may continue if you're so inclined."

"All right then, and I'm glad to know that you're ok. I…I was about to say that shady practices whenever they prop up in my organization, they're dealt with immediately and effectively. They're not allowed to fester, but I also want to make the observation that it's not exclusive to our particular industry. There are rogues everywhere!"

"Indeed," Premature weighed in after a long period of self-imposed silence, "Listen, Mr. Everyman, I've watched you berate and heap nothing but scorn on whatever my uncle said. Yes, I watched you squirm and scowl many times over, and some of the questions you raised, we know we shouldn't dignify with answers, however, in keeping with our policy of transparency and since we know we have nothing to hide, we obliged. I'll have you know, or at least remind you, that my dear uncle is and will forever be an icon in this business, and no one can take that away from him. No, not even you," she said contemptuously. "He's already made his mark on society, and what a mark," she said proudly. "What's more he's been validated by his peers and other widely respected bodies, such as Gloryland Inc., Burden Solvers Corp., Deep Sleep Caterers, Fertile Ground Providers Inc., Maximum Rest Corp., and Groundbreakers Lodgings to name a few. Even you would have to concede that the list is impressive, the best of the best. Everyman, those are who endorsed him, and as you well know, they're known for sound judgment and distinguished service, not just here but throughout the entire world. That means my uncle deserves every plaudit he's been given. In other words, he earned it. As they say, he's at the 'top of his game.' There's no award that he hasn't won, from best rookie to best reaper. You're looking at what it means to be an achiever at the highest level. Feast your eyes on him, Everyman, and learn." She followed her flowery speech by chanting, "Go I.M. Go, go I.M. Go."

Hearing her and him before and looking at them only served to make him more worked up. He felt as if he should choke them right where they were, and that feeling was more than a thought, it was over-whelming and grew into an obsession. A feeling of hate welled up inside of him that was frightening. He felt the urge to act and act right away. It wasn't a matter of toying with the idea anymore, it was action time, and he felt so driven at one point that he subconsciously appealed to an imaginary audience, asking, "Can anyone please tell me, and I do mean anyone, please give me good cause not to maul these two to 'thy kingdom come' right here, right now!" He was breathing heavily and supposedly waiting for an answer when unexpectedly and suddenly he snapped out of his rage and back to reality. Something deep within himself, some force or other checked him. That thing he later admitted to himself is called "reason." It had to be he told himself because when reality hit him, he had his hands clasped together as in a choking posture and was foaming at the mouth.

"Wha…what just happened, Mr. Everyman? For a little while, you seemed to be out of it."

"Yeah, nothing serious, thank you. From time to time I get these dizzy spells, but this only happens when I don't take my medication. I'm sure that's all it is."

"Ok, if you say so," Certain said while Premature nodded her head. I.M. figures a change of strategy could get him the result he so desperately wants. He knows the Deathes love to boast, so he decides to give them more talk time hoping that in doing so they'd incriminate themselves and reveal their true selves as the low-down scums he knows them to be.

"By the way, thank you, sweetheart for that beautiful speech," Certain says, smiling from ear to ear as he cheers his niece. He hugs her. "Well done! I couldn't have said it better myself. Bravo! Thank you again." Turning to I.M., he said, "As to my telling you about certain incidents, it wasn't as if I told you anything in confidence or you didn't already know. I thought you'd heard the latest gossip making the rounds. Everybody else has, and knowing how you delight in such matters, I led you on. In fact we both did, and from what we can see, it worked." He laughs uproariously and takes a bow in mockery of I.M. "We wanted to see what your reaction would be and now we know. We don't have to wonder anymore. It's quite clear to us you're not interested in facts, you prefer to believe the stories you've been told by other sources. It's not surprising really, you tell so many of them yourself. In your book, fake stories matter, not truth!"

"I... I've been meaning to ask, just how would you know what delights me?" he asks indignantly, "especially seeing that this is only the second time we're meeting, huh? How would you know? Are you telepathic? Or maybe a prophet? Hello, prophet Deathe," he mocks.

"It may come as a surprise to you, but I don't have to be. The answer's very simple really. It's nothing mysterious or sinister. It's called research. Maybe you've heard of it, anyway I do do research on my preys you know, oops, what a terrible slip of the tongue. Please forgive me, my...my prospective clients I should have said. Does that answer your question?" he teases.

"Maybe and maybe not. How's that for an answer? Then again please don't answer that; there's something else I'd like to say...."

"And that is?"

"I've heard about your dirty deeds, but I didn't think you'd be that barefaced to show up anywhere near here. I just don't think that anyone else would, not after they've been exposed as you have. Damn!

You're shameless. Who are you, Deathe? Just who are you? That's what I'd like to know!"

"Unlike you, Deathe is a man of his words, Everyman," his reply laced with sarcasm. "I keep them, and I'm not the Judas-type as you undoubtedly are. I told you I'd show up again, and here I am. I even predicted it would be soon, and so it is. Moreover we've got nothing to hide or to be ashamed of. How many times do I have to tell you that that's your department. Ahem," he clears his throat and continued the conversation. "As I said, they and their agents want to take our spot. That's what they're after, the most coveted spot in the business, the number one spot." He wipes away the tears streaming down his face, sniffles and says, "I'm sorry, I just can't help it. I get choked up inside whenever I think or talk about my precious niece and the great job she's done and is still doing for the benefit of our company and the industry as a whole. It...it makes me very proud of her, but it also makes me very sad to know that there are unscrupulous and unfeeling bastards out there who are hell-bent on taking her down. They prey on the defenseless all the time, and without mercy, too. They're hell-bent on destroying her, no matter the cost, and I'm issuing this solemn warning, don't mess with my niece. I don't need to tell them what the 'otherwise' will be. I won't stand for it, not...not over my dead body, not on my watch," he added defiantly. "Everyman, I don't expect you to understand how much it hurts to see and hear those wannabees launch attacks after attacks on her good name, etcetera. They're trying to drag her into the gutter with themselves, and notwithstanding the fact that I'm a God-fearing person, it still makes me harbor vengeful thoughts and resentment for them. Their actions leave a bitter taste inside of me, if you know what I mean."

Everyman couldn't help being impressed by Deathe's drama-filled performance, especially knowing it was for an audience of one. Him! But he was not convinced.

He has too many lingering doubts about the Deathes.

"It tears me up," Deathe says haltingly. "Nobody, especially when you're innocent, should have to go through what she's going through, and by extension, neither should our company. Nobody should have to go through stuff like that, let alone decent law-abiding people. Come on now. There has to be accountability, you hear me, there just has to be, period! Whatever they're accusing us of doing is not in our DNA, individually or as a company, and the scrupulous way by which we conduct ourselves could easily lead people to think we invented the word. This is a clear-cut case of character assassination, and it's there for everyone to see. This is what is called a 'classical' case and this ruthless, vicious, illegal, and relentless assault on our person, integrity, and our business has to cease. It must, and that's a promise. What's more, these are all made-up stories, fake news, and we'll expose those societal rejects for what they truly are, reprobates. No more hiding place for them! No way! The game's up and I'm putting them on notice that it is. This is a new day, and we have a new way of dealing with thugs. Our record speaks for itself and can stand up to any scrutiny, and when we said we'd expose them, that's no idle threat. That's a promise. We have names, addresses, etcetera. Some are Cold Ground Experience, Right Way Handlers, Depth Explorers Corp., Bunkers Palace Retreat, Silence Keepers Inc., Daisy Pushers and Company, and Neo Body Burners. Our research show that those are the main offenders. Yes, sir, they can't hide anymore, they've been exposed and will face the consequences…"

"So who are these people?" I.M. interrupted, his voice betraying a mix of anxiety and skepticism.

"Do you even have to ask? They're crazed, power hungry fanatics who parade as decent law-abiding business people but who are actually made up of mostly fly-by-night operators who continue to make very nasty and unsubstantiated allegations about honest and successful rivals like us and…and hear this, as I said before, without a shred of credible evidence. Seem like they have a license to smear. These people are hoodlums and the so-called evidence they're able to provide is manufactured by themselves and/or with their accomplices, yet they still continue with their stories unabated, each time making them more dramatic."

"But why, why?" I.M. asked.

"I thought I'd already told you, anyway, be that as it may, I'll tell you again. Firstly, they do so to get attention, secondly, to drum up business at our expense, and thirdly, to run us out of business, so they can take over. These are bad people, vicious people, please remember that, and don't for a minute forget that we're not talking about angels here, we're talking about evil and dangerous people. It makes me wonder how it is that we are able to train wild animals coming straight out of the forest and yet still have such a long way to go with some of our own kind. Strange, isn't it? As I've often said, they and their agents/accomplices, whatever they choose to call themselves or you choose to call them, they're generally going bankrupt or at the low-end of the industry with nothing to lose. That's another of their distinguishing feature; they have nothing to lose, no character, no nothing if you get my drift. They have or hire look-alikes in order to impersonate our more successful and high profile employees, my niece Premature being their favorite target. They definitely have a penchant for that aspect of the business, deception! They also spread false news like wildfire, using whatever means they can to do so, and I swear to you they'll stop at nothing in their efforts to destroy and displace reputable people and organizations such as ourselves. Those good for nothings and their phantom companies create and act out their own stories and quite convincingly, too. They and their functionaries pretend to be us so often that some people, the more gullible of us, start to believe they're us and that's where the confusion comes in. We have scruples, they don't. They want to take short-cuts, that's right, they don't want to go the distance or to put in the hard work and sacrifice that the business demands, and you know what!"

"What?" I.M. asked, but the way he asked and gestured sounded more like a demand. "What? What? What, Deathe?" It looked and sounded that way to him, too, but Certain wasn't rattled by it; if he was, it didn't show, and so he resumes talking.

"Much as I hate to, I have to admit, and I know I've mentioned it before, but it bears repeating, they sure have a lot of people fooled and their mischief making knows no bounds. They've introduced and want to keep questionable practices as a staple for our industry, and note this, because we stood up to them and said we won't allow such practices, we've been singled out for punishment by them. Yes! That's a fact. They know we're not complicit, so what do they do, they set out to annihilate us, hence the heightened campaign against us, a campaign that's filled with lies, etcetera. That's the cross we bear!"

"They! You keep talking about they, they this, they that. That's too vague, yo! Who the hell are they, or should I ask, who the hell is they? Is it a person or group? Which is it?"

"Don't be ridiculous! I'm being serious here and you're trying to trivialize the situation by asking stupid questions."

"I'm sorry if you feel that way, but I'm fed up with hearing about 'they' so often without knowing who you're talking about and so I have to wonder if this is a figment of your imagination, or is this for real. Your record doesn't inspire confidence, if anything it precludes it, and this is why I'd like to know if this is more lies or what. Name names! Can't you even provide me with names, and when you get the chance, please do the same for the wider public. That's all I'm asking for."

"Of course I could, but I'd be here all day just doing that, besides, and this is very important to me, I don't want to desecrate my memory or my mouth with the names of such vile persons, plus if I recall correctly you've been provided with enough names and evidence already. Were you sleeping?"

"Is that all you're gonna say?" I.M. asks, his interest heightened by Certain's explanation as to why his company's always embroiled in scandals of one sort or another.

"Here's another thing to look out for," he hears Certain saying as he cuts into his thoughts, "whenever we advertise, we do so with truthfulness in mind, and very importantly, in keeping with the requirements of the law, but when they do, they don't and don't seem to care either, hence the animosity."

"So…so let me get this straight, what you're saying is that you operate conventionally whereas they do in an unscrupulous manner and want the likes of you gone, did I get it right?"

"Exactly! Precisely! You got it finally. You've got it at last, and so I'll be real candid with you." After making that statement, he pauses, wondering if it's the right move to make as he knows the fallout would be severe if it's not. In the end, he threw caution to the wind and decides it is the right move. "There," he began, "there was a time a…a time but a very short time in the scheme of things when… when our own workers, some of them, in fact relatively few, didn't follow orthodoxy to the letter, but that was in the past, the very distant past I might add, and as I stand here today, I can say with certainty that it stays there, in the past. Make no mistake about it either, they were severely punished for their indiscretions, and for the record, some even lost their jobs; they were fired, and if that wasn't taking drastic action, then I don't know what is. Ever since our mantra has been to follow the rules religiously and our mission statement makes that abundantly clear. My…my advocacy for a corrupt-free industry is universally known and such a stance I can tell you is non-negotiable! Sometimes our detractors, the afore-mentioned fly-by-nighters as I refer to them, demonstrate before our offices holding banners with ridiculous slogans, such as Death on Deathe time. Death to the Deathes, etcetera."

"Well, well, well, Deathe, another confession, and what else do you feel the need to confess? Don't be shy, spill it, you know as well as I do that you have a lot of confession left in you. I say spill it pappy, I'm listening, and maybe, just maybe, we'll get the truth at last."

"So you want the truth, eh, Everyman? Well, ok, here it is, we didn't intend to discuss certain elements of the business with outsiders such as yourself simply because we didn't think you especially have the capacity to understand, and you've just proved us right. Can…can I say something to you privately?"

"I can't stop you, so go ahead."

"Thank you, sir. Just let me whisper in your ear, please, it's personal."

"All right," he says disgusted. "Go ahead I say."

"If...if they were giving out prizes for being dumb, you'd be at the top of the list."

"Get in the car assface," they ordered in unison as if they'd rehearsed the line, all this as they walked out the door with him sandwiched between them.

"Say, I.M., didn't you tell me not too long ago that you wanted to move, or was I hearing things?" Deathe asks laughing.

"Yes, I did," he answered feebly.

"Well, quit stalling and get in the damn car. You wish is about to come true."

There was a brief scuffle after which Certain said, "I'm sorry it had to come to this but I'm awfully glad that nothing serious happened in that no one was injured, and as I've often said, we're here to serve as best we can, and that's why we decided to take you to your new home right away. We figured there'd be no point in waiting, and while we're on our way, tuck in your shit!" he barks. Turning to Premature, he says gently, "sweetheart, please give him a hand, will you."

"Sure, uncle," she says. "I'll be glad to."

I.M. pushes her hand away and says, "I don't need your help, I'm capable of dressing my own self. Get your murderous hands offa me!" He turned to Deathe and said, "I guess I'm what they call 'old school', huh?"

"I guess so," he says smiling in admiration of I.M.'s spunk, even at this hour.

"That's the spirit, old man," he says.

Right after that exchange, the Deathes said their goodbyes with happy smiles registered on their faces while that of I.M.'s was a picture of gloom. The whole thing lasted just a few minutes, but it seemed like eternity to him. It was bizarre and other-worldly, almost as if he was bought and paid for by those people, the Deathes. That's how he felt, as though he was their property and couldn't resist their bidding, no matter how absurd or how hard he tried.

TO MOTHER

To Mothers everywhere
To your Mother
To my Mother
To Everybody's Mother
It's Good to know
You have your special day
And doggone it
That day is today
Hip hip hooray
From the north to the south
You deserve a big shout out
And from the east to the west
We all say you're the best
So let's all join in
And say happy mother's day
Not once, it bears repeating
Happy Mother's day

TO FATHER

Dad stand up and take a bow
Salute! Your time is now
Step out of the shadows
You belong in the light
You've been protector, provider
And so much more
And without you
I'd not be here for sure
Put that smile back on your face
It so reminds me of the word grace
And know this, for me
You'll always be
The man
Happy father's day.

TO MOM and DAD

If you should rewind
Here's what you'd find
The refrain, no fussing
And no fighting
It didn't take only one of you
It took both of you
To make this dream, me, come true
And if you go forward
You'll be going toward
The refrain, no fussing
And no fighting
It didn't take only one of you
It took both of you
To make this dream, me, come true

7

Wake Up Call/Recollection/Hope

"Mr… Mr. Everyman, um, um, Mr.Everyman," he heard a voice calling his name. "You're a lucky man, a very lucky man I might add."

"What? Why? How? Who? What are you talking about, man?" he asked confused. "And…and who are you anyway?" He was still groggy.

"I'm Dr. So and So."

"Dr. So and So," he repeats, trying to concentrate. "Where am I, and where is my regular doctor?"

"Dreamland General, and she's on vacation."

"Dre…Dreamland General? I don't understand. How did I get here? Why am I here?"

"Slow down, you'll have all the answers in a little while. You're here because you had a fall, and you could've seriously injured yourself you know."

"A fall?" he asks anxious to hear more.

"Yes, and maybe it was a good thing it was from the couch and not the bed."

"Why is that, doc?"

"Why is what?"

"The bed and couch thing. After all a fall is a fall, right?"

"Yes, but from the bed, it could've been more impactful seeing that…."

"OK, doc, I get it. The height from the bed to the floor would be more than from the couch to the floor. I get it, no need to explain further."

"Good, that's ok, but remember you asked. Secondly, your emergency alarm system alerted us; good for you that you have one. Because of it, our paramedics got to your home in a matter of minutes. Unfortunately, once there they had to break your door down to get to you. Thankfully, your condition wasn't as serious as they initially thought; they found you on the floor seemingly still dazed."

"So I fell from the bed you say?"

"Oh, no! From the couch I said."

"What else, doc?"

"It was reported that you were writhing, moaning, groaning, soaked in sweat, and screaming at the top of your lungs, "Let me go, leave me alone, parasites. Oh, no, I'm not going anywhere with you, leave me the hell alone I say. We're done here, go away, get out now. If you don't, I'll call the cops. It's as if you were struggling with someone or something. That's what I was told."

"Seriously, doc," he said, looking around nervously as if he expected "others" to be there, and for a brief moment, he'd forgotten he was at the doctor's office and not at his own address. He remained rattled and asked, "Did they say whether they saw anybody else in the room with me, doc, did they? Do you recall? Please tell me, doc," he pleads, cold sweat pouring out of him. He was scared out of his mind.

"No!"Doc answered emphatically. "Should there have been?"

"As a matter of fact, yes!" he answers with a tremor in his voice. "I had visitors. Two of them, an uncle and niece team. They must have hidden or ran away when your team entered."

Doc strokes his chin.

"That's strange, nobody mentioned seeing or hearing them, muuh, muuh. Do you even know them?"

"Yes, doc, unfortunately I do. They're the Deathes!"

"The who?"

"The Deathes!" he says again, only this time with a frown.

"The Deathes," he repeats astonished, "what funny names. That's extraordinary. I've never heard of them before, not in the circles I move. They must be from out-of-town." He scratches his head and shakes it from side to side as someone in deep thought is prone to do. "Nope, I've never heard of them," and he contends that it's unlikely he'd forget the owners of a name like that, even if he tried. He called it "unusual." "I've got to hand it to you though," he continued.

"Hand what to me, doc?" he asked confused.

"Well," doc said, "you've got to admit that you sure seem to have some strange-named friends. Must be a new trend."

"They're not my friends!" he said bristling. "They're acquaintances at best and very recent ones, too."

"Oh," he remarked simply.

"Yes, that's all they are, and even that is a stretch. They claim they're known and highly respected internationally and have issued an invitation to take me to 'a better place,' and why? Because as they put it, they 'like and admire me very much.' They also say they like the work I do, and they're ardent supporters who want only the best for me. To that I say that's nice, but as tempting as the offer sounds, and it is tempting, I've never not ever asked for or accepted any help from them, however, they keep insisting that I go to this new place with them." He sighs, "They seem determined to take me there."

"Is that so?" he asked with raised eyebrows.

"Yes! and do you know what else they said?"

"No! Tell me!"

"They said they're gonna re-locate me to a new place that's worth dying for, how sweet," he reports excitedly. "That's how exclusive the neighborhood is I understand."

"You don't say," he says curious.

"Yes, I do say," he answers with an air of self-worthiness.

"That's some kinda special fans you've got. Geez, what wouldn't they do for you. I guess it's flattering to know you have such adoring fans, eh? They're so devoted and that's so cool, mauh, muah, muah!"

I.M. shrugs his shoulders and says, "I guess it comes with the territory, you know, celebrity, success, etcetera, the usual." He smiles sheepishly and says, "You know how that is!"

"Or maybe they're groupies, and if they are, don't you find it a bit flattering, the way they follow you around," he goads.

"There you go with that word again…"

"What word?"

"Flattering!"

"Oh, I'm sorry if it annoyed you. I'll try to avoid its use in the future."

"Getting back to this groupie query, frankly, I don't know who they are and what they do besides what they tell me, and I was thinking about moving to another place for a multiplicity of reasons long before they came into the picture. It's just become more urgent due among other things to the string of successes I've had over the years. The desire has always been there for somewhere else you know, somewhere more private and exclusive but I don't know enough about those people, and just in case you're wondering who I mean, wonder no more, I'm talking about the Deathes. I just wouldn't leave such arrangements to them, complete strangers. Besides, I've already decided that whenever I'm ready, I'll go the usual route."

"And that is?" he asks.

"Through a licensed real estate agency of course. There's absolutely no room for the Deathes, no matter their maneuverings, plus I don't know exactly what it is, but I have a gut feeling that there's something sinister about them. They're almost never in a subjunctive mood, they're nearly always in an imperative mood. You know what I mean, doc?"

"I think I do."

"Yeah, they seldom ask me what I want and mostly tell me what to do, and I don't like that. They're too bossy, and simply put, I don't trust them!"

"Good for you, can't say I blame you. So a pair of would-be kidnappers, huh?"

"I...I guess so, doc, one never knows, especially with the way things are going these days...although..."

"Although what?' he asked leaning forward.

"As I recall, they referred to themselves as harvesters."

"Harvesters, is that what they say they are?"

"Yes, doc, I'm sure of it," he answers.

"Mmmmm, I wonder what it is they harvest. Did you ask them, eh? Do you know?"

"Yes! I did ask them, and after dodging the question for some considerable time, they reluctantly relented and said souls."

"Souls!" he repeats, trying as hard as he could to figure out what exactly did they mean by it. "My guess," he concluded, "and this is nothing more than a guess, is that in a roundabout way, they were saying they were preachers. That's slick," he says with a chuckle, "real slick. Give them their due, that's pure genius, that's what it is. Damn!"

"So maybe it was a good thing that while we were engaged I tried talking to them in a good-natured way, right up until they grabbed my arms and tried to take me away to the so-called 'better place.' For me that was when they crossed the line. I kid you not, doc, some people have some kinda over-inflated egos and the Deathes, sad to say, are prime examples, but to me, the really frightful thing is that they wanted me," he hits his chest Gorilla-style, "to genuflect, and me," he hits his chest again, "to be obsequious. Imagine that! I let them know in no uncertain way that they have the wrong guy. Yes, sir, I did."

Doc cleared his throat, "Ahem," then he said, "Let's go back to when the Paramedics first arrived at your apartment..."

"What about it, doc?"

"Well, they said when they asked you what had happened, you appeared to be out of it, shrugged your shoulders, and said you didn't know. You weren't sure. You remember?"

"I," he laughs. "I wasn't being uncooperative or anything like that. Honestly, I wasn't sure, and I told them I needed some time to collect my thoughts and there's no question I was out of it. I really and truly was."

"Well…" he said pregnant with expectation. He was anxious for a more detailed account.

"Well, what?" he asked as a way of stalling, but doc wouldn't let him.

"Now that you've recovered sufficiently and seem to be back to your normal self, and since I've brought you up to speed with what little I know, I think you'll agree with me that it's my time to get some answers. Don't you agree?"

"Answers to what, doc?" he asked with raised eyebrows as someone who's surprised would.

"Well, let's see. I'm interested in knowing what brought about your fall. You did fall, didn't you?"

"Yes, doc, I did, but it's not really as mysterious as it sounds. I mean, I wasn't inebriated or anything like that. I didn't even have one drink, neither did I pass out because of any medical condition. I was sober as sober can be. I do remember having a very light snack just prior to falling asleep though and I remember having a dream, that's all."

"A dream! That's interesting! What kind of a dream, do you remember?"

"A very bad dream," he responds. "It was scary and I'm glad it's over."

"That must have been some dream," doc surmised. "Wouldn't you say so, Mr. Everyman?"

"You think, doc?"

"Do you mind telling me what it was all about?"

He laughs and says, "If I do, you'd probably think I'm crazy."

"How so? Wh…why would I think you're crazy?"

"Because the dream itself was bizarre," he explains, then pauses to collect his thoughts before adding, "It was frightening and it really hit me hard."

"In what way?"

"It's kinda hard to describe. It...it was like a kick in the gut, wham! Or a knockout punch, pow! It's like no other experience I've ever had," and with that said, he slowly and painstakingly recounts the dream filling in bits and pieces as he went along. Finally, he says, "It felt so overwhelming, so vivid, so real and drawn out, I thought it would never end. I...I get chills all over every time I think or talk about it. Sometimes I even pinch myself to see if I'm really still alive."

"Oh, yes, you are, there's no doubting that, thankfully, and it's my hope that you'll stay that way for a very long time."

"Thank you, doc. Hallelujah!" he shouted enthusiastically.

"I'm alive," he says more subdued and less certain despite doc's assurance, and that's because he's still traumatized by the unsettling dream he had. It still leaves a lot of unanswered questions, even though he now knows what the Deathes mean by calling themselves "harvesters."

"I don't know what to say, except what a story! What you had wasn't just a dream, it was a nightmare!"

"That's exactly right," he says with a sigh of relief, glad that it's over.

"Your story touches the lives of everybody, young and old, abled and disabled, rich and poor, etcetera. Tell me about your childhood."

"Well, doc, there's not much to tell. Except for setbacks, it was very 'normal.'" He reflected for a moment. "I also liked to read and ask questions, that's about it, oh, oh, as well as participating in different sporting events until injuries kicked in. I was even considered good and worthy of further development."

"Any brothers and sisters?"

"No, I was an only child, and except for mom, dad, and me, our family wasn't close-knit by any stretch of the imagination. I hate to say it, but for a favored few, nobody knew or cared what the other relatives did, how they lived or where they lived. Contact was minimal at best or non-existent if you know what I mean!"

"I do unfortunately," doc answered. "So you say you lost your parents how again?"

"In an awful accident," he replied, wiping away tears, "and it's extremely painful to even think about it. It's…it's one of those memories you'd like to erase forever."

"I know it is," doc said as he wraps, consoling arms around his shoulders. "If you don't want to discuss it any further, I'll understand."

"No, that's all right, and since we're on the subject, I might as well carry on. So I was twenty-two-years-old at the time and the accident involved two buses traveling at night in opposite directions on a lonely stretch of dimly lit, winding and wet country road. It was a brutal head-on collision taking the lives of the driver of the bus my parents were on, as well as several passengers on both buses including my parents. The other driver took off on foot and that was the end of that. Nobody saw or heard anything from or about him since. He just vanished."

"How tragic," says doc. "I'm sorry, so very, very sorry."

"Thank you," he replied, and after much thought, he says, "and now I hope we can get back to the personal question you said you wanted to ask, although I'm wondering what could be more personal than what we just discussed."

"You're so right, what we just discussed was very personal, wasn't it, anyway, pardon me, what I want to know can wait a while longer, so let me start by making a few observations. You're now a senior citizen, very successful, and have been for quite a while, rising from virtual obscurity to national and worldwide acclaim and to top it all off you've brought to light a story that everyone can relate to, no matter their station in life. Congratulations! And this leads to the question I've been yearning to ask."

"Which is?"

"How come you don't have a family?"

"Aha! I know that was coming, and by family, I suppose you mean a wife and kids, huh,am I right?"

"Bingo! Exactly!"

"Well, over the years, I've dated different people, but I wasn't looking for a permanent relationship, besides not everyone is suited for that role," he says contemplatively.

"So you're telling me you're not suited?"

"Now maybe but certainly not then. There were a multiplicity of other factors too and while I don't want to sound 'preachy' I felt that life isn't something you should gamble with. To me it's sacred, and ever since I was a teenager, I realized that having a family without adequate preparation was a no go for me. I'd seen enough unnecessary suffering around me and had learned some of the causes, and so I tried as best I could to avoid such causes like the plague. I knew even then having a plan was key. I wanted my family to have the best life possible and I knew that wishful thinking by itself wasn't gonna do it. I lie to you not, doc, I respect life so much I was willing to wait until I could properly maintain a family, even if it meant adopting in the end."

"So what about now?"

"Doc," he laughs and he laughs hard, "are you kidding me? You've seen my chart, haven't you? That nuclear family ship has sailed for me. All I'm looking for now is an aide-one that will be around, around the clock, especially given what just happened to me. That's… that's one of the main reasons I'm searching for another place, which I think I mentioned before. I also plan to build a vocational training school, so I'll have lots of children after all."

"Sounds good to me, old timer. Good luck, Mr. Everyman, and pleasant dreams this time."

"Thank you, doc, same to you, and bye."

Everyman had his discharge papers, but before going, he and the doctor smiled, then laughed, embraced, and patted each other on the back and he remembers he'd heard something somewhere about "will and way" and he knows for sure that he has the "will" and he sure hopes he'll find the "way."

9 781649 135179